Born Winner:

The Highs and Lows of

Mike Vaz

MIKE VAZ

Born Winner: The Highs and Lows of Mike Vaz
Copyright © 2019 Michael Vaz

Books may be purchased in quantity and/or special sales by contacting the publisher, Michael Vaz, by email at mikevaz29@yahoo.com.

Cover Design: Seymour The Painter
Instagram: Seymourthepainter

Formatting: Tanisha Stewart
www.tanishastewartauthor.com

Editing: Tanisha Stewart, Liv Clement, Nick Clement

First Edition

Published in the United States of America
by Michael Vaz

Acknowledgements and Dedication

First and foremost, I thank God. Without Him, I would not be here today. I dedicate this book to my mother and father, my grandparents, my siblings, the rest of my family and friends, and the city of Springfield as a whole, including Mayor Sarno, who has served as a great support.

There are so many people that I want to acknowledge that it would be impossible to name them all. I appreciate everyone who has had an impact on my life, from my childhood years, to now with my injury.

Some of my teachers that had a positive influence in my life are: Mrs. Grimes, Mrs. Lockett, and Mr. Stroughter. I also had some great coaches, like Coach Mendel, Coach Kozol, and Coach Moe. I also extend my gratitude to the Martin family, the Maloney family, and the Clement's. Each of you have had such a profound effect on me.

I would also like to thank the doctors and nurses that treated me, as well as the physical and occupational therapists. They were truly God-sent. I could not have made it without them. To the entire staff at the Spalding and Baystate facilities, including Baystate's Emergency Room team and ICU unit – I truly would not be here without you.

To Nicole Maisonet, it's hard to come by genuine love when you are in my situation. Thank you.

To my barbers, Choco and Cheto – I will never forget the day you helped me make history, being the first person to ever get his hair cut in the ICU. Much appreciation to you for coming through for me.

Synopsis

There were over 200 people in the waiting room of the ICU that night.

A local legend. A dual athlete.

What happened to Mike Vaz?

Hear the story from his eyes. Delve into the mind of the dynamic and multi-talented man that took his high school and his city by storm.

After suffering multiple gunshot wounds that led to his paralysis, most who hear this story would think that Mike's story was over.

But he is here to set the record straight.

He is here to demonstrate that you should never count anyone out.

Born Winner: The Highs and Lows of Mike Vaz takes you on a journey through his life - his childhood, his sports career, his scandals… and the fateful night that almost led to his undoing.

Table of Contents

Born Winner:

The Highs and Lows of

Mike Vaz

MIKE VAZ

My Father's Birthday

It was February 8th – my father's birthday. He had passed away 10 years prior.

I was drinking and reminiscing about the times we had shared. At around 11:00 or 12:00 o'clock, I decided to go lie down. My girlfriend at the time was already in bed. Her three children had been asleep for hours. I heard a loud noise in the back of the house.

Immediately, I felt a chill down my spine.

Something wasn't right.

What I heard had sounded like a gunshot.

I went downstairs to see what was going on.

When my foot hit the bottom step, I heard somebody coming.

I went back upstairs and hid the oldest child in a closet, along with his twin siblings, who were infants at the time. I made sure that they were safe, then went back to the staircase to face the intruder.

From the top of the steps, I saw my girlfriend's ex-boyfriend, the father of their children, standing at the bottom.

I asked him, "What are you doing here?"

He looked up at me and said, "I came here to kill myself."

I tried to redirect him.

"Brother, you shouldn't even be here. What's going on with you?"

He started to approach, bounding up the steps two at a time.

Adrenaline began coursing through my veins. I knew right away that it was about to be on. As soon as his foot hit the top step, we were fighting. I got the best of him. He fell down the steps and I heard something loud fall out of his pocket.

It sounded like metal, and I knew it was the gun.

I heard him cock the hammer back.

Time froze.

Somehow I got inside the room and tried to shut the door. He shot through it. It made me back up. When I backed up, BOOM. Another shot hit me in my right arm. The door opened and he stood behind it. He still had the gun in his hands.

I didn't have time to think about pain.

My autonomic system was in overdrive as I launched myself at him.

We began tussling for the gun...

A lot has happened in my life since that night.

But before we get into the details, let's begin where my story started.

BORN WINNER: THE HIGHS AND LOWS OF MIKE VAZ

Chapter 1: My Childhood

In the Beginning...

MY UPBRINGING MIGHT NOT FALL into what some would consider 'typical' in American society. When I was younger, my parents, Yesena and Mike Senior, struggled with crime, drugs, and poverty.

When they were coming up, drugs were everywhere. It was a constant in their everyday world. In fact, it swept through communities across the nation at a rapid pace and affected countless families across the board. Today, it is referred to as the 'crack epidemic'.

Along with dealing with the realities of drug use and abuse, my mom and dad – barely out of their teens – had a child almost every year, for a total of six children.

I was the oldest – the first-born. I was spoiled. My parents took me everywhere. That's why I'm still in contact with all of my dad's close friends and associates to this day.

When I was growing up, everybody treated me like I would be the one to fill his shoes. They looked at me like I was local royalty, just because he was so well-known. His reputation preceded him.

Despite my dad being in and out of jail, he still played a strong and positive role in my life. It seemed like he just got stuck in bad situations – caught up in the streets like many others. When he was a teenager, he was trying to make ends meet by selling drugs. He was trying to support us.

God-Given

Despite my atypical upbringing, I've always been into sports.

I'm a natural athlete – it just came easily to me. In elementary school, my athletic ability first surfaced in an unusual way. I used to do backflips at lunch time for the girls. I would take my shirt off, go in the back on the grass... I'd get a couple of my boys to go back there and we'd just be flipping for the girls. That's where I started to get all my athleticism from.

I also did dance – I went to Kick, Step, Kick. It was a dance class at the South End Community Center in my hometown – Springfield, Massachusetts. That was the first dance class I took. I had a natural rhythm.

I used to think I was Michael Jackson.

Dance class only made me better.

Plus, all the finest girls were enrolled, so you know I was in there.

Good and Bad Mentors

According to the stereotypes, based on the fact that my dad sold drugs and was in and out of jail, most people would probably think that I would end up taking the same path. Not true for me. My dad always encouraged me to stay out of the streets and to do something positive with my life.

Even though my mom had her own struggles, she taught me to do the same.

My mom, my dad, and my grandmother were like a triple threat in their own way. They each influenced me to do the right thing in life, and to not allow myself to fall into bad decisions. Having a strict grandmother at home definitely helped. Any wrong I did, everything was taken away. No Sega Genesis. No watching Michael Jordan play the game. If I couldn't see my Mike games... I would be in my room doing hella push ups. Mad at the world. Beating up my little brother. My little brother got the worst end of this.

Because I grew up in an urban area, I had all types of influences around me. One of the first lessons I had to learn was how to separate my home life from street life, and street life from friends. There is so much that goes on in the type of environment I grew up in that I had to fall back and learn how to observe and make wise decisions for both my present and my future.

I was surrounded by both good and bad mentors.

Pat Stroughter was one of my good mentors as I was growing up. Pat Stroughter was the health and sex ed teacher at Kiley Middle School, and he coached the basketball team. He and a couple of guys from my grandmother's church also served as positive role models. Pat was one of the few people that could get my grandmother to let me out of the house. She trusted him. My grandmother didn't trust too many people. My grandmother didn't like too many people. My grandmother didn't allow us to go places with too many people. She was a very strict woman and didn't play about her grandkids.

Me and Pat had a dope relationship; something like father and son. He actually introduced me to the world of women. Pat was a real life player. He would take me with him after practice after school to go visit the girl's team. If one of the moms he was talking to had a daughter, I would be entertaining the daughter. That was like my first experience chilling with girls. It was dope. I knew I was learning from Pat's good example. That made me a ladies' man, for real. Between 7th and 8th grade, I watched how Pat interacted with the moms, and I took notes.

But my mother, father, grandmother, and Pat weren't the only influences in my life.

Some kids my age were already choosing the street route. Trying to get money over anything. I wasn't against it - it just wasn't the route I was trying to take. I knew what I loved - sports. I would go to the Rebecca Johnson School and I would see all the local dope boys doing their thing. My observations of the different situations they found themselves caught up in showed me how to keep myself away.

I never really had anyone try to steer me in the wrong direction – I just saw different things that I knew would harm me in the long run, and I tried to stay away from them.

Football, My First Love

From the first time I picked up a football, I fell in love.

My first experience being on an official football team was when I played in my hometown of Springfield at 5-A. It wasn't necessarily the best experience. The coach had preconceived notions about who I was. I don't know if he didn't like my step pops, or whoever my mom was dealing with at the time, but from the start he treated me like dog shit. The whole set-up was kind of ghetto, to be honest. He was basically torturing almost all the newcomers. He would line us up and make the older guys run at us and hit us.

I said, "Man, this is not for me. I am *the hell* out of here."

It got to the point where the coach was angry at me for some reason, so he singled me out and had all the older guys on the team run at me – full speed.

I told my mom what happened. She said I didn't have to go back.

Once I hit middle school, I took my talents to South Beach, aka Chicopee Massachusetts, to play for Coach Chuck and the Chicopee Braves. Chicopee is a mostly white town. I was the only Black kid on the team and they treated me like royalty. They actually showed me what I should do as far as the game, and how I should do it. Despite the fact that Coach Chuck was so strict, I was able to learn that way. It stuck. It made me who I am today. It made me a better player. I owe it to Chicopee Braves for honing my craft.

The Braves taught me structure and discipline, and how to play various positions. They also broke things down in a very detailed way. It was a night and day difference from my experience with the Springfield team. Since I was already a raw athlete, I was able to pick everything up easily. They were setting me up to be a problem for the remainder of my football career. I was a beast.

From my experiences with the Braves, I would definitely say to parents who have young children that are interested in sports to start your kids early. I learned so much about football and life just from playing sports, and it only set me up for great success in the future.

I can't wait to start implementing that advice in my own family.

I don't have any children, but I do have a nephew. He's one. I can't wait for him to at least get four or five. I'm going to start him doing all types of drills and training once he gets to the right age. I want it to be instilled in his brain, like *I have to work out. I have to do all this to get better.* Once you do that, it just makes a player way better. Once you instill that work ethic – work ethic is 90% of everything. That's what's going to get you there. Work ethic. You have to be committed to everything you do.

Basketball Also Has My Heart

I know I talked a lot about football being my first love, but basketball definitely has my heart too. I owe my skills on the court to my middle school English teacher, Mr. O'Reilly. He had an eye for spotting talent. He saw something in me and encouraged me to play basketball. I'd messed around with it a little bit, playing pickup games at the Martin Luther King Community Center and the family center on Acorn Street, but I wasn't really serious about it, until Mr. O'Reilly took me aside.

He said, "You look like a basketball player. I understand you play football, but you could definitely be a basketball player. Mike, you can really go far with this, if you want to."

From that point on, he took me under his wing.

I'll never forget him.

He was one of my favorite teachers. He would bring a ball into class. One day he did a demonstration and showed us how he could dribble. He was like a Steve Nash. Once I saw him do it, I definitely wanted to do it too. He started teaching me. He started showing me stuff. He was getting me more and more interested in basketball.

Once I developed the skills and knowledge of the game, he sent me to my first intensive camp experience at the Springfield College Basketball Camp. From then on, I was turned out. I loved it. I couldn't put the ball down. I quickly learned that with basketball, you could carry a ball with you everywhere. Unlike football, where you need somebody else to throw it back with you, all you need is yourself and Spalding to improve your game in basketball.

We lived with my grandmother for most of our childhood, and wherever my grandmother went, even if it was a trip for the church or a retreat, I brought a basketball. My basketball was like a permanent extension of my body. I just kept improving as the days and years wore on.

I was getting better and taller, better and taller.

By my eighth grade year, it was craziness. That's when we started the eighth grade basketball league at Springfield Middle School. The league had existed before, but it didn't pick back up until the year I hit eighth grade. It was probably the best league ever. Me and a bunch of my boys played together. One of my best friends, Alexi Garcia, he was my point guard. Then I had my boy Ivan Dodds, rest his soul. He passed away. My boy Marcus also was with us, and a bunch of other dudes.

We were nasty.

I was averaging 45 to 50 points a game as an eighth grader.

I was killing every other school there was.

Rebecca Johnson, New Leadership, Duggan...

There were some great, great games. We played Chestnut in the championship, and we beat them. They got so mad, they messed up our locker room. They were throwing chairs and stuff and breaking glass and everything. We killed them.

It was dope.

Our group of players continued to excel in the game. Everyone in Springfield basically grew up together. If you didn't play with them, you played against them. You could tell who was going to be nice, who wasn't... Who was going to link up. It was crazy how me and some of my rivals from Duggan all linked up in high school at Commerce. Even a couple of guys from Chestnut. It was pretty dope. I loved basketball just as much as football, once I started playing.

I said, "I'm going to play both of these! I'm going to try to get nice at both of these!"

And that's what I did.

I got nasty at both sports.

Eighth Grade Year was Epic

Playing two sports kind of opened the door for me to get picked up by recruits either way. I excelled at both basketball and football. My summers, I was playing basketball. My winters, I was playing football. So that's how it worked out.

My first official basketball team had the same high quality training as my first official football team. I was a fast learner. It came to me like second nature. I was a raw athlete already. I had a six-pack in sixth grade.

Eighth grade year was epic.

Because my stats were so impressive, I was seen as a 'stand out' player.

That's how I ended up getting 'recruited' by certain high schools. Central wanted me to go there. But there was only one team that really stood out, and that was Commerce. The head coach was at a couple of the middle school games watching me. It was pretty dope.

Going into my freshman year, the coach actually came by the crib and took me out for pizza. He kind of persuaded me to go to his school. He also took me shopping for school clothes. It wasn't supposed to happen, but he made it happen. He gave me a credit card and told me, "Don't tell nobody."

I didn't tell anybody until now.

His tactic worked – I committed to Commerce, without a doubt. He sent me home with two big party sized pizzas for my brothers and sisters. My grandmother loved that. Once you get my grandma happy, you got me.

I'm all set.

I was signed, sealed, and delivered.

Chapter 2: Family

My Momma Made Me,
My Grandma Raised Me

I KNOW I'VE BEEN TALKING A LOT ABOUT SPORTS, but I want to step back a little bit and talk about my family. My family is very important to me - they made me the man I am today in many ways.

One of my life lessons was to always respect and care for your family. Always instill love into your family. That's major. If you do it, you will prosper. I feel like as long as you keep the whole family together, you will all understand what it takes to function as a unit. That's what my mom and grandma focused on. How to make it.

Once you start separating and losing each other, there's no family values.

There's nobody to help bounce back with.

Everybody needs a place to fail.

They need a place where there's somebody there who will heal them. It's hard. Some people don't have that type of emotional support system.

Whether it's violence, drugs, fights, or anything else that happens outside of the home, you can't control it. What you *can* control, you have to direct it the right way. And keep it right.

When I was younger, we got taken away from our parents.

My grandmother Emma stepped into their place.

As I mentioned previously, my grandmother was very strict. She was a devout Christian lady from Panama. My mother gave her permission to adopt us so we could all stay together. We weren't scattered around Springfield in different foster homes, getting sent here and there, but instead we were able to stick together.

My grandmother kept us together.

We lived with my grandmother from when I was eight until about eighteen. My grandmother held it down. Limited funds and everything. But she made sure I was acclimated.

Despite the fact that my mom, Yesena, struggled with her drug use, she never missed a game. She would have boyfriends, and whoever she was with at the time, she would make sure they helped to take care of us. With my dad, Michael Vaz Senior, in and out of jail, my mom's boyfriends would buy me sneakers or whatever I needed for sports, and that's how we did it.

Can't Forget About My Pops

My dad was always locked up.

It definitely had an effect on me, because he wasn't always able to be around to be a direct influence in my life, but like I said before, he still played a strong role in my upbringing.

My father would always tell me, "Stay away from this," and "Stay away from that." My dad and me had a really good over the phone and visitation-type relationship. I learned a lot from him. And he wasn't even around.

I wasn't trying to follow society's perceptions – that if a father was in and out of jail, that his son would be also. I refused to follow that cycle. My father ensured that I didn't go down that path.

My father was the head inmate for Behind the Bars. It was a program to help youth stay away from jail. He was mentoring kids my age. The local kids would come back from doing Behind the Bars, and be like, "Yo, I met your pops. He was a cool dude. He told me – we looked at his cell. He had all your articles – everything about you, posted on his wall. All he thought about was you, and what you are doing, and how positive you are. Look at what you're doing, with your dad being locked up" they would tell me. "Keep it up, because you don't even know what you are doing for other people."

Those words really helped me put things in perspective.

I would hear so many kids my age come back and have so much respect for my dad. That made me have respect for my dad too. Even though he wasn't around, he was kind of impacting me as a father from afar in a way. Some kids don't have any connection with their pops period. That was how I connected with mine.

If my father would have played no role whatsoever in my life, I know things would've been different for me. In a bad way. I would have been a street dude. Knowing he was guiding young dudes living like we did made me realize that every opportunity, both good and bad, was right there in front of me. Negativity was always within arm's reach. I could have run away from Grandma's house millions of times and taken the easy way out.

I just wish my dad could've been there in there in the flesh day to day.

At the end of the day, one thing I know for sure is that a dad being there for you means something. I really don't think I'd have the mindset I have today about my situation if it wasn't for my pops and the way he carried everything.

To all the father's out there... Your kids are listening.

Double the Family, Double the Fun

Growing up in a household like mine, with my mom and dad not being our sole influences, was difficult at times. When we were first taken away from my mom, we used to be at the door at my grandmother's house saying, "They're coming to get us. They're coming to get us. We're going back with them. This is just temporary."

My grandmother Emma understood what we were going through, but she didn't let us dwell in our pain. She used to do different things to purposefully make life fun for us. She made sure we played sports and that we went on vacation every summer. She would take us down to Florida and Virginia... We went to Disney World once... She made sure we enjoyed our childhood, and she made it a point that we enjoyed life to the fullest.

I'll never be able to repay her for that.

And while they weren't always around like most parents, my mom and dad did their parts too. They both did what they could to show us that they still loved us even though they couldn't necessarily be there for us the way they wanted to because of their issues.

Love is all that matters at the end of the day.

It keeps you going. Even though they were constantly battling through shit, we had an unbreakable connection with our parents. And that's beautiful, because it doesn't always happen that way. In most cases with people where we're from, the parents are just gone and you have to try to find them when you get older. Like I said before, my mom made it to every big game. No matter what, she made sure she was there. That was dope, and it's something I'll never forget.

Me and my siblings stayed with my other grandmother (the great Erlene Ingram), and my grandfather (Grandpa Willie Poon, rest his soul), during the summers. They used to always play the numbers. I remember that shit like it was yesterday.

Things were different at their house.

They were much less strict than my mother's mother.

They let us play outside much longer and didn't have nearly as many rules.

We loved it.

One thing my Grandma Erlene taught me about was cashing in cans. I used to love that shit. We used to go around and collect cans wherever we saw them, and she had a station wagon that we used to fill up and go cash them in.

Every once in a while there were good payouts, and the hustler that she was, she made sure we got paid. She would always go get me a little toy or something or just give me a couple bucks. She made me realize the value of the dollar. If there's no hustle there's no paper at the end of the day. I get my gambling habits from her too though…. But I stay winning.

My grandmother on my mother's side is a Seventh Day Adventist. We could not stay out past the time that street lights turned on. If we got in trouble, our privileges were taken away – no basketball, no video games, no nothing.

There was this one time that I was supposed to be at work, and I told my grandmother Emma I was going, but instead I called out went to basketball practice.

I don't know how she found out, but when she did I was waiting with the team in the hallway to go into practice. She starts screaming my name, "Michael!"

And she's got like a real distinctive way of saying it.

Everyone on my team was like, "Yo, that's your Grandma."

I said, "I know!" and I had to run down there.

She made me leave practice and yelled at me in front of everyone. I was pissed at the time, but now I realize why she did handled it the way she did.

I know my grandmother's structure and discipline helped me become who I am today. She kept us all involved in community organizations, events, the Martin Luther King Center, and Shiloh church for a reason. She saw the big picture, and sometimes kids growing up like we did are never blessed with the opportunity to see things from our elder's shoes.

I'm thankful that I was.

My grandparents weren't the only family members that stepped up to the plate.

My Uncle Cooper was the one who really showed me what life was all about. He was the realest dude I ever met. He showed me how to put my first condom on when I was 16, and this dude used a Budweiser glass bottle to do it. He called me over, a little drunk, and to this day it was one of the most funny experiences of my life

He was like, "I know you probably out here doing things but you better be strapping up! Your grandmother will kill you if you bring home a baby."

He used the bottle and slid the condom on, giving me a visual demonstration.

That was just one of those things I needed from like, a father-figure with my dad being locked up all the time. He stepped up and gave me that breath of fresh air. My Uncle Cooper also always gave me a couple bucks whenever I needed it – he looked out for me.

He was pretty dope.

As I said before, my whole family played a strong role in my upbringing. I have a very close-knit family on all sides. Everyone watched out for me and my siblings. I was also close with my Auntie Divette and my Auntie Sheila. They were my mom's siblings.

My aunt Sheila was very supportive. She went through some of the same struggles as my mom, but she taught me how to hustle and to do what I needed to do to survive. Both she and my mom were strong role models for motivation in life.

My Uncle Junior – God rest his soul – was my mom's brother.

He was the real business-savvy uncle. He showed me how to buy houses when you get enough money, and how to invest. He was also a real heavy gambler, so he showed me about the Roulette tables. That's why I think I'm addicted to Roulette. Uncle Junior was multitalented – he built his house from scratch. He was so smart.

My dad and his siblings unfortunately dealt with incarceration from time to time.

Oftentimes they were sent to the same places. I used to go visit them a lot. My mom was very heavy on me going to visit my dad. She made sure me and all of my siblings saw him. She tried to keep a nice relationship between us. That was really important, because a lot of times you will hear stories of kids who never get to see their incarcerated parent at all, and then you don't even know them, and it's weird when they come home.

But my dad wrote me a lot. He was an artist, so he used to draw pictures of everything. If I had an article in the newspaper, he would draw it and send it back.

It was pretty dope.

Back to my grandparents.

With my grandmother on my mother's side, Emma, as I said before, we could not be out late at all. I had to beat her home sometimes. I used to sneak outside all the time, and I would see her van coming down the opposite side of the street.

I had to run home and do some Olympic jumping to the front porch and slide into the house before she could see me. I used to always make it though. I was so good at it. If she would have known, I would have definitely gotten a whooping.

On my father's side, summers used to be the best time in my life. All my cousins on my dad's side were there. They were all my age, so it was a lot of us. One of my uncles had 16 kids. My cousins, the kids from the neighborhood, and I used to play outside all night on Eastern Ave. I also grew up on Tyler Street and Pendleton Avenue.

My Cousins

On my mom's side, I grew up with my cousins Tirra, Desira, Dwayne, Eric, Christina, Bianca, and CJ. We all basically stayed at my grandmother's house. Everybody was there. We used to have all the picnics and cookouts. We was all tight. All of us. We were all around the same age. That's what made us really tight, too. We stayed that way from childhood through to high school. Even now, mostly all of us have kids around the same age.

We try to raise our kids to be close how my grandma taught us.

I have nothing bad to say about any of my cousins. They all had a big part in my life growing up, and still do now.

One thing about all my cousins on my dad's side was that we could flip. So we used to have mattresses set up everywhere off of Eastern Ave.

My boy Darnell used to have a big double backyard. We had like ten mattresses set up back there. It was like the ghetto Olympics. We were really good at flipping. We would flip all day. Back flips, back twists... We would be nice.

We didn't really compete, but we would go around to different hoods and different hills and flip. There was a big hill at Brookings School. It was like a 20-foot hill. We used to flip down it. Whenever they were building new houses in different places, and there were dirt mounds in the back, we would go back there flipping. It was dope.

Young Blacktop

I also had a bunch of friends on the Ave growing up. When I went to spend summers with my Grandma, my cousins on the Ave were: Money Mike, Poobi, my cousin J-Rod, J-Dog, Durant, DJ, Body, Elton, and Gotti the Gator. We were a real tight clique. It was all of us.

Young Blacktop.

It was crazy. We used to do everything together.

We used to get mattresses and bring them to Darnell's crib – Gotti Gator, and we would have two different setups. Then we had more across the street from J-Dog and Elton's crib in the middle of the field. We also used to have mattresses in a field at one of the abandoned houses on Tyler Street. It was amazing.

We all played a game called Ring-A-Leave-Ya at night.

It was me, Corey Parks, and my boy James. It was a game like Manhunt. There were two teams with two jails. The object was to catch the whole other team and lock them up.

We did from Pendleton Street all the way to Lebanon - a span of a couple blocks. You had to go all over. It was night time, too – like 11 or 12 o'clock at night. It was massive fun. This was before when Springfield was genuinely fun at night time.

You didn't have to worry about shooting and people driving by and all that stuff.

This was when the Ave was the best spot to be. There was so much going on, from Pendleton projects down to King Street, Lebanon, and Eastern Ave.

Then when I went back to my Grandma's house (Grandma Emma), I used to chill with all my Sycamore boys.

Daniel Woods/Woody Rock (rest his soul), Ali Phatts, Quick/Keshawn Narcisse – he's my cousin too, Lighty/Kevin Smith, Little Dust Po, and Little 5th. We also had Aquan and Jamee – they were the Karate Kids. They loved old Kung Fu movies. That's all they thought about. That's all they did. They used to practice that.

My boy Ali Phatts is truly one of a kind. We used to play basketball at Rebecca Johnson school together, and he always loved to rap. He performed at various places, including the Harambee. As an adult, he is still into music, but now he does it with his son.

It is so amazing to see his trajectory – being the young guy with long hair down to his butt, rapping in front of an audience, to now being a grown man with a son who is following in his footsteps. I am so proud of my friend.

I also wanted to share about my cousin Little 5th - Tyrell. Little 5th was a great kid. He used to come to my house all the time and chill with me. He looked up to me - kind of like a mentor or role model. He would ask me different questions about college, seeking for advice. He saw that I was making it, and I was from the same area that he was from. I served as an inspiration for him.

He was nasty at football too - he played for 5-A. He just couldn't get away from the streets. You can't take the streets out of anyone, when they grew up in it. Little 5th actually had a lot of promise due to the fact that he had a solid skill-set.

Unfortunately, he never got the chance to live his dreams.

The story went that one day, 5th was out with his boys. A shooting occurred.

He ended up losing his life.

His death really hurt me, because he was a young guy with a lot of ambition. His dad had been heavy in the streets too - he was something like a legend, and 5th was known by everyone to be following directly in his father's footsteps, along with being gifted at sports. He was only 16 when he passed away.

His death really hurt me, because he really could have made it.

More about my Sycamore crew.

Even though I wasn't necessarily around them all year because we were split between our two sets of grandparents, the Sycamore kids took me in just like I was one of them.

Me being an athlete, I always had my solidified spot.

And I wasn't no bitch.

I wasn't scared of nobody. I wasn't intimidated. I was going to hold my own. I was going to speak for myself. So they took me in like a brother. And we would do the same thing I was doing on the other side of town.

They knew I had the basketball courts in the back of my house, too. Even though my Grandma Emma was strict as shit, she had me set up with two basketball courts in the backyard. So I had a full court. Everybody loved my backyard on Oak Grove.

Oak Grove was the shit growing up.

My God-brother and next-door neighbor was Kevin Smith, aka Lighty. He was crazy. He used to go steal dirt bikes and bring them back to the street. He would come back with like three of them. We were the first kids on the street with dirt bikes.

We were riding and zooming and cruising. It was dope.

Those were my childhood friends.

My Siblings

As far as my siblings - I was the oldest of six kids - four sisters and one brother, then I had two step brothers and two step sisters. We are all close. All of my siblings came to all of my games. All my cousins came too. My family supported very strongly.

I felt loved and I believe it made me play better.

Growing up, I always felt that I was leading by example, showing my brothers and sisters to not get in trouble with the law all through high school.

My brother Keon used to play video games. He also played sports, but he enjoyed the video games more than the sports.

My step-brother Sharvin came into my life a little later, but it didn't make a difference. His dad was Claude Brantley, aka Fiddler – God rest his soul. Fiddler taught me a lot. He was a witty guy who had a deep voice and stayed fly. Everybody used to always say, "You gotta face the Fiddler."

He was a solid dude. He would always have a bag full of quarters, and me and Sharvin would go cash them in and take the money to Six Flags. It was epic.

Me and Sharvin's bond grew more and more as we got older. When I got injured, he used to stay with me all the time. He answered the phone whenever I called, and he is still here for me as a support to this day.

All of my sisters were also very supportive. Growing up, I was super protective over them. They're my heart. Michelle, Ebony, Latoya, and Shaday. They are all in a row in age.

Michelle is the oldest, then Ebony, then Latoya, then Shaday.

When we were growing up, I made sure I never let anything happen to them. I was really big on being a protector and a dad for them, so to speak. A major part of my life was to never let my sisters get exposed to anything street. I am so happy that none of them ended up with any stupid baby fathers or boyfriends that messed with them or beat them up.

They knew I was not letting that happen.

They love me so much.

And now that I am in this position, they take care of me.

They make sure I have everything I need. Especially Michelle. Whenever I was sick, she would come down and stay with me. When I was going through some mental stuff, she came and got me right with the Lord. She helped me get baptized. More about that later.

Michelle is really deep into church. She's really serious. She's got two girls and she's married to a man named Brandon. He's a really cool dude. They met in Virginia. He's a God-fearing man as well. That's all that matters in our family. Michelle is my rock.

Latoya is my little fighter. If any chicks ever did anything to me, Latoya would be ready to get LIT.

Shaday is my little baby girl.

My sister Ebony has two kids. She has my first nephew. Ebony loves sports, just like me. We bonded over it. She would be the sister that would want to come sit down and watch a game with me. She also played basketball. My grandmother had my sisters playing basketball just like me when they were younger. They all have a deep love for sports, but I know it carried on for Ebony now that she is older.

Ebony and her boyfriend talk about sports all the time. They go to Celtics games... We're big New England fans, so they are Patriots fans, Celtics fans, Bruins fans... Anything around New England, they love it.

But I'm an Eagle's fan. Die hard Eagles fan.

Mike Vick, McNabb, those are the dudes I follow.

My family and I have huge feuds over football.

When the Eagles played in the Super Bowl, and my team won, they were all mad. My whole family are Patriots fans, so they were pissed at me.

I was loving it. It was glorious. Everybody was salty.

The Springfield Community

I can't forget about my community. My city showered me with so much love throughout my life that I consider many of them like family too.

The church my grandmother went to – Shiloh, also played a strong role in my development. I learned through the church how to be a man that took responsibility for my wrongs and strived to be a better person than I was yesterday.

I played a lot of basketball at the church with all the deacons and the older guys. They instilled a lot in me. They helped my grandmother out. John Johnson was one of the major influences. He definitely taught me a lot, along with my cousin JR, Harold Green.

My grandmother was an usher, and a lot of the usher ladies helped out too. They knew she was taking care of all six of us. We would eat a lot over people's houses. It was cool.

The school nurse at Commerce, Sue Lovotti, also played a strong role in my life. Me and her daughter are still friends to this day. When I was born, I suffered from lead poisoning. Sue was one of the nurses that helped treat me. When I got to Commerce, she said, "Oh my God; I was at Wesson Women's when you were sick as a baby, and I helped take care of you when you had lead poisoning!"

So we connected from that.

Our bond continued to strengthen all of my four years at Commerce.

My brother Keon played basketball and football like I did, and loved them, but he was more into video games. He was a running back and a cornerback. He played at Agawam High School and Commerce High School. Sue Lovotti actually took him in for a couple of years just to help my grandmother out after she helped me through high school.

She was really like part of the family.

The Springfield community was always supportive of me growing up.

I have much support from my city.

I love Springfield, and Springfield loves me.

Our games used to be packed with Springfield residents coming to support. They would always be sold out of tickets. My city would love seeing me play. I was a breath of fresh air. I was the new Travis Best. They showed me mad love.

That's one of the reasons I am writing this book, to shed light on the love and support we have in Springfield. We get overlooked a lot, but we are the birthplace of basketball.

A little city in Massachusetts.

We need our respect.

We have a lot of hidden jewels out here, but we don't get sought out too much. Boston gets the most recognition. During high school, I had to actually go play my AAU basketball seasons in Boston to be seen a little more, because Springfield doesn't get enough recognition.

Chapter 3: High School

So, What's the Hype About?

AS I MENTIONED BEFORE, I ENDED UP joining both the basketball and football teams at Commerce High School. Since I was basically recruited straight out of middle school, I already had somewhat of a reputation among the older players. I had played with the Chicopee Braves during middle school, and we actually won a championship together. A lot of the guys I came in with as a freshman, we also played 5-A together.

I had played 5-A for a year, then I went to Chicopee Braves and played for three years.

Commerce had a pretty good football team already.

My freshman year was basically about them seeing what the hype was all about.

Their answer came quickly: We took Commerce by storm.

We had a bunch of studs: Me, Laheim Johnson aka Chef, Darnell May, Tee Baymon, and Jordan Toomer. We

had probably one of the best freshman classes in the last
fifteen years. We came in strong. We were killing all the
other teams. We actually got to play a lot of varsity as
freshmen, which was unheard of for most of the guys,
because they weren't big enough or strong enough. But we
came in, and we were all built different.

The class of 2003 was built different.

We all came in looking real strong.

They let us do all the workouts with the older dudes.
They saw that we kind of blended in, and me and some of the
other guys looked better than people who had been there for
three or four years already.

The coach was so surprised. He loved it. It was epic.

I was a huge freshman. I was 6'2 coming into my
freshman year. I was 185-190 lbs. It was really, really dope. I
took full advantage of it.

The season was good. We made it to the Super Bowl. I
actually got to play in the Super Bowl my freshman year, and
I picked off a pass from the other team and ran it back for a
touchdown. I was the only freshman to score in the Super
Bowl.

It was epic.

I made history.

I was making history as soon as I got there.

We won the Super Bowl. I got a Super Bowl ring, so
we thought we were the shit. We were freshmen, and we
already had Super Bowl rings.

As for basketball, during freshman year, when
basketball season started, we were football players, so we
had to go to tryouts a little late. When we got there, the coach

pulled us all to the side and said, "You guys don't have to try out. I already got my varsity team named and ready."

I was the only freshman that was playing varsity at that time. Everybody else had to play JV. The first six games, I didn't start. But through practicing and playing hard, I earned myself a starter spot by the seventh game of the season.

We won a lot of games.

We made the playoffs.

Unfortunately, however, we lost in the second round of the playoffs to Cathedral. Cathedral was nasty at that time.

Once that season was over, AAU started for the summer. We had a sick AAU season that year. I was playing with the Jaguars. I played for the Martins.

The Martins are a local family – they're white, and they're pretty nice at basketball. My Grandma Emma loved them. She would let me go with them no matter what. They were responsible for me. They definitely helped me and molded me the right way. They took me in under their wings, and helped me become a man.

We played in Tennessee and Florida against top players in the world. It definitely helped me gain an edge. I felt that in my sophomore year, I would be unstoppable as a result of the experience. I played against elite athletes like Carmelo Anthony and JR Smith.

AAU was epic.

Me, Nick Stafford, and Brian Kelly were the only Black kids on the team. All the rest were white boys. Pat Martin, Russel Martin, Brian Burke, Nick Wichels, and Ryan Maloney – Ryan's one of my best friends.

His family was from Granby. I met them at my first tryout when I played for an AAU team with the Martin

family. Ryan and I hit it off from the first day, and we have
been friends ever since. Not just him, but his whole family.
His dad, Dickey, his mom, Brenda, his brother Steve (God
rest his soul), and his two sisters – his youngest sister was
my biggest fan.

The Maloney family loved me so much that I had my
own room at their house. I even lived with them once briefly
after high school.

They embraced me like a son and a brother, and I saw
them the same way. I showed them my culinary skills, since I
was used to cooking for my brothers and sisters growing up.

Their home was like a safe haven from the drugs and
gun violence that was prevalent in Springfield.

Ryan and I also of course bonded with basketball. We
each scored our thousand-point games on each other. It was
epic. His family came to all my games, just like they did his.

His little sister even got a signed trading card from me
– the school nurse, Sue Lovotti, had some made for me.

During the AAU season, we all played really good
together. Our chemistry was so dope. I was the muscle and
the wild one for them because I was the black kid that didn't
care. I was gonna stick up for them. I wasn't going to let
nobody bully my white boys.

Pat Martin was a deadly shooter. Ryan Maloney was
my point guard. He was a deadly shooter too, but he had a
little more handle to him. Russ Martin was a hell of a
shooter. These were all my boys growing up, freshman year.
We were so tight.

A Dual Athlete

My sophomore year was about learning myself as a star - a dual athlete, and exhibiting humility - I was cool with everybody; I liked to make everybody laugh.

That sophomore year, the quarterback was hurt, so I had to step up, and that's the year I became King of Commerce. That's when I became the man. I started taking over big time, playing football. I was the quarterback. I was the lead guy. I was calling the shots as a sophomore. It was pretty dope.

That's what kind of made me into a leader. Sports made me a leader. I was always naturally that way. I don't follow nobody. I call my own shots. I feel like that's the way you gotta live in life. Don't let nobody really tell you how to live your life. You gotta be a leader.

Sports helped me to be a man. With me already doing it at home, helping to raise six kids, I felt like I was a leader no matter what. It was pretty dope. And the coach gave me a lot of leeway. He let me call a lot of the plays sometimes, and I figured out what was good for us to do.

The older guys took a loving to me.

The way I carried myself was more mature than a lot of kids.

I didn't act all foolish and corny. I was more of a laid back, old soul type. That's basically how you could describe me – I was a young dude with an old soul. I always kept it that way since I was young.

I just tried to blend in, and make myself known through my play. I let my play speak for me. I didn't really have to say much.

When I came back to play for Commerce after the summer… At AAU, you play against elite competition worldwide. Then you come back to little old Springfield. I was feeling like Magic or Michael Jordan out there compared to kids around here. It was like a cake walk. I was killing them. We had a dope season that year. We made it to the playoffs again. We lost in the semifinals. That was my breakout year in both sports.

We didn't win the Super Bowl in football as sophomores, but we had a hell of a season. We ended up losing to Ludlow. We made it to the conference championship in basketball, and we lost to Cathedral that year too.

Learning Responsibility

I also learned some great lessons about responsibility as I was growing up, and these lessons carried into my high school career.

Life made me grow up.

While I was in high school, I worked a few jobs. First, I worked at Big Y as a bag boy, and I used to push the carts. Coach Mendel helped me get that job for my Grandma's sake.

Grandma Emma said, "You ain't gonna be able to play sports if you don't have a job! I'm not buying those basketball kicks!"

So that was my job to get my sneakers and stuff.

That's another reason I love my grandmother. She instilled in me a strong work ethic from day one. If you didn't do your chores, you couldn't do anything.

When I was younger, I used to have to hand wash socks. If your socks and underwear were too dirty, you would have to hand wash them in a bucket. She gave all six of us a bucket. We each had our own.

We used to have dirt in the backyard where we played basketball. So we used to put on double socks because they would get super dirty. If they were really dirty, you had to hand wash them. Grandma was not putting those with her clothes.

Back to high school.

My second job was at a local hospital.

I worked there for two-and-a-half years. My aunt was supervisor in the kitchen, so she got me a job down in the cafeteria. I was down there bussing carts and washing dishes. I was moving through the hospital.

I used to have a lot of sex in the hospital too, with my supervisor and a lot of girls. There are a lot of private bathrooms at the facility that no one goes to. There were a couple of coworkers I used to have sex with in these bathrooms, along with my supervisor.

I was loving it. I was a nympho. I couldn't help it.

It was a part of me, and I embraced it.

While I was having my fun, I was also building responsibility.

I would bring home a nice check, so I got to get all the Jordan's I wanted. All the school clothes I wanted. That kind of made me feel good. It definitely helped me stand out and get to school better.

My Other Interests

One other thing about high school: We had a video production class. I loved it. One of our teachers used to be a newscaster. He was okay. There was another younger teacher that I liked better, but he ended up leaving to go work at like News 22 or something.

I also enjoyed drama class. Any type of role I could get into, I would kill it. Acting felt like a second calling, in addition to sports. My drama teacher, Mrs. MaCarthy, was my dog. I loved her. She used to just let us have fun. I used to love doing improv. I love to make people laugh. I still do it to this day with SnapChat. I got little videos on there. I will see something really quick, and then I will make a video out of it. I use the little filters they give you. I really want to get more into acting and drama in the near future. Even in a wheelchair, I wouldn't mind doing it.

My High School Friends

I had a lot of friends during my high school career. One of my first best friends at Commerce was Gus. He was a driver. He used to come pick me up and bring me to all the parties. He had a little red car. I'll never forget it. Gus was my guy. He made sure I got to everywhere I needed to be.

Games, tournaments... He was there.

That was dope.

Next was my boy Ray J/Ray Carter.

In the morning, walking to the bus stop, I used to meet up with him. We would go to his sister's house and watch the movie *Above The Rim*. That was his favorite movie. He knew every word from it. I used to go watch it with him every day. That was dope.

Ray J had a broken leg one summer.

His ass was still on the basketball court, killing it. When you're a little kid, you don't want to stop playing, no matter what. He had a full leg cast on, playing ball.

That shit was the funniest.

Then we got my guy Brian Kelly. He used to always come over my house. He had the bike. He was a little smaller, but he used to always be with the big dogs. So we let him ride with us.

Brian Kelly was my boy. We used to chill and ride bikes everywhere. Wherever we went, we were on our bikes. We were always going to courts to play ball or at open gym at Rebecca Johnson. Rebecca Johnson was the spot where all the local kids were playing ball all night. You could also go swimming in the back. It was open every summer. That used to be the best thing.

Blunt Park swimming pool used to be flooded. That's where we used to have back flip contests in the grass. It often got intense. If you couldn't flip, you could just step to the side.

It was a process of elimination, and it usually boiled down to me, Lil Tupac, and Jozel. They were kids who were nice at flipping. We used to do little games with it. That was dope.

I'm still either cordial or friends with most of those guys to this day.

I'm still me, so everybody still continues to treat me like I am. They don't look at me like no sob story or none of that.

Another way I met friends at Commerce was through my role as sort of a student ambassador. When new students came to the school, I had the honor of walking them around and introducing them to everyone for whatever class they were in or whatever team they were on.

One person I introduced to everyone was my boy Plastic, aka John. John was very creative – he actually now owns his own clothing line – Gypsy Clothing. I remember the first day I met him. The principal said, "Hey, this is Mike Vaz, our star athlete."

I walked him around.

He was like "Damn, man! You know everybody! Everybody likes you. You cool."

I made all the new students feel good.

One of my other best friends came from New York.

He was a Dominican named Jairo Tagara. That was my boy. He was straight from the city. Lil Harlem Shakin ass dude. He was a pretty boy, but he blended right in. He stuck with me and my crew. He ended up playing football, and earned a Super Bowl ring with us. He was a cool dude. We're still really tight to this day.

All my football teammates, basketball teammates… I still talk to all of them. Even my Boston dudes, Dorian Brown and Dwight Brewington – Dwight's deaf but he was actually nasty. We also had Antonio Anderson – he ended up playing for Memphis, then his eye got messed up, so he had to stop. He's doing really good now. He's coaching a really high class AAU team.

Every college I went to, every college party I went to, I'm remembered as 'that guy'. The cool dude that came and didn't start trouble, and stopped a bunch of bullshit that was about to happen. That's what I used to do. I was that guy. I was always trying to make sure that everybody was having fun. Everyone loved me for that, so that's why I embraced it so much.

Even to this day, it's still mostly the same way in a wheelchair.

Ain't nothing going to change.

I'm still a party promoter, still at the games talking to the kids... I'm never going to stop that. It's instilled in me. It's like my calling. What God has me out here to do. I would be dead already if He didn't have another plan for me. I'm pretty sure this is a part of the plan.

It's a blessing to be able to help somebody else out.

Even if they are in a better position.

Just by looking at how I handle my life, and how I take it day by day and don't change. I don't fake, bend, or break. That's just my motto. Live by it, die by it.

Back to my friends.

My high school best friends were Little Richard/Richard Freeman, Warren Fluellan, aka Scoop, Jairo, and Gus. We were always together. Those were like my best friends. Scoop and I used to always get into trouble together. In High School, he was in Special Ed classes, so I used to go get him out so we could chill. We experimented with different styles of clothing, and we even made some of our own clothes.

Scoop used to work for his dad, cleaning offices downtown. I would go with him after practice and help, til I got my own job – then I would help on my days off. We were always getting into something. Always somewhere partying with Richard, Jairo, and Gus.

We actually took a trip during the season to All Star Weekend in Atlanta our senior year. We got back too late to play in the game, so they made us sit down. We ended up losing to Central. So that kind of hurt. Otherwise, we won two Super Bowls together. We all went and bought the same Jordan's and wore them. We did some dope shit.

We used to get all the girls together, too.

I Was a Household Name

By my junior year, Commerce had taken over western mass. After not winning any championships for football or basketball during sophomore year, I went into my junior year like, "I'm not going out like a sucker this year."

We delivered.

I was a household name.

I was in the newspaper frequently for both football and basketball. I was a premier athlete, but my grades were suffering. This caused problems for college - they took advantage of my athleticism.

The lesson I learned from that was to stay focused on books and school first. The coaches didn't care about grades - they cared about winning. I would encourage kids nowadays to stay above average in their grades - grades are important for scouts to see when they start looking

In football season, we went undefeated and won the Super Bowl that year. That was my second Super Bowl. We were killing it. Undefeated the whole season. Nobody could say nothing to us in Springfield. We was the shit.

Then in basketball, we made it to the semi-finals, but lost that year again. So I really couldn't get over the hump in basketball.

I wasn't really mad at the losses in basketball, because football was my first love. We won the Super Bowl in football. I was already proving points where I needed to prove a point. That's how I looked at it. Basketball was like the icing on the cake.

I was nasty in basketball because I'm a raw athlete. I could do that.

In AAU that year, we went to Nationals again, but I switched teams. I went and played for the Boston Metro team. They were more elite and played in better tournaments. I was competing against the top players in the nation. I was playing against guys like Melo and Corey Maggette. A bunch of dudes that were going to the league. There were a lot of dudes from down in Georgia. California also had a dope team that year.

There was another Boston team – BABC. We played against them and beat them. We had a bunch of dope dudes. They had some good guys too. Mike Jones... I can't remember many other names from that team.

For those who may not be familiar, AAU is how they recruit for college athletes. If you're really nice, you can also go to the NBA or even overseas straight from there. Nowadays, AAU is taking over the world. The recruiters have their eyes on different players. There's a top 100 list that they have for every state. They rank certain kids – it's really competitive. I was ranked pretty high on their list as a sophomore, junior, and going into my senior year.

A Local Unicorn

My senior year was amazing. I was a local unicorn.

In our first game of football, we lost to Longmeadow, but I had 17 tackles in the first half. I ran for a touchdown, threw for a touchdown, and caught a touchdown pass – well, intercepted a touchdown and ran it back. I had a hell of a game. That was our first game of the season – our breakout game.

Then we were undefeated for the rest of the season and won the Super Bowl.

I won three Super Bowls during my high school career.

It was a dynasty. No one else has done it since.

In basketball, we got to the Western Mass finals, then lost to Amherst. It was a good game. We saw our mistakes, learned names of a lot of recruiters from local colleges and big name colleges - Minnesota, Syracuse, Richmond, Florida, everybody.

Academically, I slacked off with my grades again.

When you are a star, you tend to get away with stuff. Looking back at my academic situation, I would tell student athletes to take help that is provided, whether via tutoring or otherwise. Don't get lost in stardom. Keep school first.

My senior year was also a time of reflection. I reflected a lot on what all my experiences made me in the past 3 years. I was without my pops. He did Behind the Walls with young guys, which was good, but I didn't have him in my life as much as I wanted to.

I ended up getting Player of the Year in both sports that year.

We went to the Western Mass Championship and lost again in basketball.

I couldn't get over the hump.

We made it all the way every time, but we didn't win the final championship.

But I won in football. Football was really my main sport.

A Ladies' Man

My high school sex life was also amazing, because I was a standout freshman.

All the senior girls were feeling me. They were showing me love. I was getting it from all age groups. My first high school girlfriend was an upperclassman that showed me the ropes, so to speak. She used to come pick me up and we would get in her car and get busy in the back seat. I lost my virginity to her. This was after my uncle showed me how to put on a condom.

I was well prepared.

Freshman year was full of fun.

I used to mess with mad chicks after her. It was like a marathon. Everywhere I went, I was getting it. I'm a chameleon. I'm able to talk to chicks. That's one of my key traits. I got a real gift of gab. Women love me. I'm a funny dude, and I'm easy to talk to, and I listen. Chicks love when a guy listens, so… I learned that at an early age.

I was putting up numbers all the way through high school.

All the older chicks were loving me.

Sophomore year, I was messing with another girl, who was actually going out with the point guard from our rival school's team.

I had to step up and intervene in that.

One game that we were playing against Central sold out. One of their star players fell in front of the bench where all the girls were sitting.

I reached out my hand like I was going to help him up, but then when he reached up to grab my hand, I said, "No, no, no!" I ran down the other side of the court.

The audience said, "Ooooh! Ooooh!" Because that was their star player, and I dissed him.

I got that from *Sunset Park.*

People loved it, and I ended up dating the point guard's girlfriend for a while after that.

The star player I dissed used to like her too, but she wanted me. I beat them in the game, and got the girl. I was winning on all sides.

Despite the fact that I was in high school, winning all these games and getting all these girls, Grandma Emma still had a tight grip on me.

I was going through a lot growing up, but I had a good situation.

Grandma Emma wouldn't really let me leave the house much, so whatever chick I was messing with, they had to have a car so I would be able to sneak around with them.

There was a vacant lot across from my house. I used to park on the side of the vacant lot, and that's where I used to get busy. I had to keep my eye on the porch, so if my grandma came calling for me, I would run back into the house. I never got caught. She never even suspected me. I was too smooth. I did that all through high school.

When I turned 18 in my senior year, it was no holds barred.

I was everywhere with chicks. Everybody knew that about me. I was always about chicks. Basketball, football, and girls.

I also used to love to travel with my girlfriends.

Every girlfriend I had, I traveled with her. Everywhere. Every summer. I was never around. That's why people respected me. Guys looked up to me. They were like, "Bro. I see you on Facebook. On social media. You're everywhere."

I had about seven to eight stamps early, many of which were courtesy of one of my high school girlfriends. I had been to several countries before a lot of other people, and I'm only 34. I have a lot of experience going to different spots around the world, and being loved wherever I'm at. My attitude is timeless, and the way I come off to people, they love me. Genuinely. As soon as they meet me, they take a liking to me. It's like a whole experience in itself. I love that about myself. I can adapt to any situation and make it good.

I can have an amazing time.

It's all about life, and making it the best with what you can.

The Love of the Game

Back to sports.

I had three types of basketball games that were epic for me during high school: Central vs Commerce, Cathedral vs Commerce, and Holyoke vs Commerce. Those three games, from my sophomore year to my senior year were always sold out because everyone knew that there was crazy competition and that it was going to be a good game.

Our gym wasn't that big, so we would sell out quickly.

Despite that, it would still be packed. Even if we played at another gym.

I didn't necessarily have big moments in basketball or football – it was big games.

Although we played hard against each other, there was no real animosity between the athletes on the different basketball teams. We were friendly enemies. Nothing serious.

With football against Central however, that was serious. We shared the same field because Commerce didn't have its own field.

We had to let them know that even though it was their field at their school, we owned it.

We had more wins, and they never beat us on it.

Those were my biggest games, playing against Central.
I used to do everything I could do to beat them.
I never liked to lose against Central. And I never did.
Every football game I played in against Central, we
won. Except for one.

It was in my freshman year.

The only game I lost in basketball to Central was in my
senior year and it was because I went to Allstar Weekend the
weekend before that Monday. I came back too late that
Monday, and Dr. Henry, my principal, sat me out because it
was against the rules to come back after 12 o'clock on a
Monday if you had a game that day.

She was one of a kind.

She was strict.

All of my Super Bowl games were very memorable
because I scored in every Super Bowl I played in. Senior
year's Super Bowl was amazing, because I scored in three
different ways. I caught a touchdown pass, I ran for a
touchdown, and I threw for a touchdown. So that was epic;
me being able to do that all in one game.

My Scandals

I can't properly end this chapter without talking about
my scandals.

In high school, two of my best friends were white.
Andy Owens, and my boy Ryan Maloney. They used to take
me out to Holyoke. Not the hood Holyoke; the Mount Tom
Holyoke. The beautiful part. You would be like, "Man, how
the hell did I get out here? This is nice! These big houses,
swimming pools in the back yard... I'm in heaven." I was
out there in heaven.

One New Year's Eve, he took me to this white chick's house. We were over there chilling, drinking... I already knew she took a liking to me because he told me that she said to bring me over. So I go over there and we are chilling.

All of a sudden, the mom comes from upstairs with a bottle of wine. She's already half drunk. She looked at me like, "What are you doing here? You look too old to be hanging out with my daughter. You're too handsome."

I was like, "Aw, man... I don't know what's gonna happen, but it might be something going on here tonight."

So, the night is going on. Everything is winding down. Everybody's getting tired. Everybody starts to separate themselves, dudes with girls... I knew the chick. She wanted me to stay with her. I ended up saying, "Let me go to the bathroom."

I go to the bathroom, and guess who I run into? The mom. In a drunken mess. She was in the bathroom. She jumped on me, ripped my shirt open, and she basically took advantage of me.

I was about 16-17 at the time.

I just went with the flow. I was like, "How can I say 'No' to something I don't know about?"

So I ended up having sex with the mom and then staying the night with the daughter.

So it was a mom-daughter combination.

The Mom knew about everything, but she ended up making breakfast for everybody after that. The daughter didn't find out I slept with her mom until years later.

Another story.

I had graduated high school and went to a bar called the Keg Room. It was downtown on State Street in Springfield. I went with one of my older friends who used to come and take me out. I was nice and saucy. I saw one of my old teachers from high school there! She was one of the baddest teachers ever.

One of my favorite things to do is to talk about something and to talk it into existence, or tell myself, 'I'm going to do this', and end up doing it. I always get it done. That's one of the things I do, and I love about myself. I used to do it with all kinds of things like dunking and throwing accurate passes, and other things.

When I was in high school, I told myself that I was going to get that teacher when I was old enough. The time came that night.

I saw her at the bar. I was nice and drunk so I went up to her and started dancing with her. I was telling her, "You know, I always wanted you. Every time I saw you in class, I used to dream about you. I knew it was going to happen."

Her husband had passed away a couple of years prior in a freak accident, so she was a widow.

I was old enough, she wasn't married, and we were both consenting adults.

She told me that she thought I was very, very handsome. She had a couple of glasses of wine. One thing led to another. All of a sudden, the night came to a close. I ended up at her house. My boy dropped me off. I told him I would call him when I was done. I never called him. She brought me back to the crib. I got her done. I knew it. I told myself I was going to do it, and I did it.

Chapter 4: The Streets

Stacking Coins, Racking Points

AS IF THAT WASN'T ENOUGH, I WAS ALSO out here in these streets playing basketball.

And making money, might I add.

That's how I made my living. Off of drug dealers betting on games and buying me sneakers. All the local drug dealers used to pay me to play ball. They used to buy my sneakers and they used to treat me good. They used to bet on me, and bet on my teams, pay for my team's sneakers, pay for us to do everything. I used to love it. That's why I love the hood. The hood always treated me good.

A lot of them were mentors, friends, older people in the local community. They took care of me. That's why I love trying to give back to my community. Trying to do stuff to help the community move forward from all the gang violence and gun violence.

This happened all through high school for all summer tournaments. I used to win almost all the summer tournaments around here. My street record is pretty impeccable.

There was a league called the Hubbard Park League. I won that for six straight summers with my team. That was when I was a little older. I was in my 20's.

That's been going on for years.

Sometimes you had to pay a fee to get in a tournament, and sometimes there were cash tournaments where you could win money at the end. Those tournaments were really worth it.

One time there was a $10,000 tournament. We played pretty well, but we lost. We played against some big names. Cliff Davis, a couple of older NBA players, Speedy Claxton, a bunch of dudes.

I went to Ben Schoolfield, Hubbard League... I used to kill it, because after AAU, I was so much better than everyone around here. It made me so good. That's why everybody knew me on the court.

I don't think there's a lot of dudes that did what I did.

We used to put together our own teams. Me and a couple of my boys. My step brother Little Richard used to play for teams. All the local dudes that used to get money used to take care of us. It didn't matter where they were from. If I was on a team and the money was right, I would play.

I needed a pair of the best sneakers that were out.

I used to collect Jordan's, and they used to buy them for me. Everybody knew that.

That was straight love.

Some of the regular street ball tournaments out in Springfield would pay sometimes depending on who you played for, just because they didn't want to lose. In the streets, you get clout off of your team winning basketball tournaments.

There were also dunk contests. There was one in Boston that I won. It was called the Sprite Dunk Contest. It was me against this kid Will Blalock. He played for the Detroit Pistons later on in his life. He won a championship with them. I played against him in the finals. I put the ball between my legs, then I did a standstill windmill and I won it.

He came up to me like, "Yo, that was crazy!" He couldn't even think about trying it. It was that hard. He just gave up – gave me dap and said, "That's your trophy. That's your money."

I was a junior in high school when that happened. That's crazy.

Blalock definitely elevated his game after that contest.

It Didn't Stop in MA

There have been basketball tournaments all through the northeast – Springfield, Boston, Connecticut… But I played with my same core guys: Ray J, Smitty, Rome, Andre Roberson… Brian Kelly used to be either playing or coaching, Yousef, Jamal Warren… We used to tour from city to city, state to state, and winning, ever since we were sixteen.

My boy Yousef inspires me to this day with all that he does. He hosts the City of Guards, where he has all the best guards come together and play against each other at the Hall of Fame. It's epic, considering that Yousef is also one of the best guards I ever played against in Springfield.

He, Brian, and I were unstoppable in our street ball tournaments.

That's how we got our names.

Whenever we would go to Boston to play in a $10,000 tournament, they had NBA players, they had players from overseas... It was a dope situation.

We did all this with just a made up Springfield team. We were all the best players in Springfield at the time.

Brian Kelly was more of the organizer, and I was more of just the heart of the team. He never lost that gift – he actually became quite successful as an AAU coach and a Collegiate coach after he graduated college. He has won numerous championships, and does everything he can to give back to his community. Some of the kids he coached even ended up in the NBA!

Brian and I actually played football and basketball together from 5-A on up through high school.

Brian had his own set of tragedies, just as I did.

He was involved in a serious car accident that claimed the life of his cousin Joe (God rest his soul), and he almost lost his life as well.

Thankfully, he is okay now, and he does all he can to inspire kids in his community.

We all do – Brian, Andre, and I.

When we played in tournaments, I was the guy that would make us go. If I was amped up, everybody followed. I was something like a captain.

I was the intimidator, the motivator... because I ain't take no shit. I was big, Black, and sweaty.

Andre, Kelz, and I were also big on the party scene. Sometimes we would go play two games back to back in whatever state we were playing in – New York, Connecticut, Massachusetts… Then after the game, we would shower and still hit the club later that night. We were full of energy.

We were known as those guys. Athletes.

Of course, it came with its perks.

We would go to parties and compete with each other to see who could get the most girls. Once we each found someone and were done partying, we would head out with our girls and end the night off right.

Andre played on a different high school team from me and Brian, so we were technically rivals, but that didn't hinder our friendship. Andre is still our boy to this day. He's doing well – living in Baltimore with his girlfriend and his kids.

We found out about these street ball tournaments through AAU and through growing up, whenever we would go out to parties and different places, we would hear about them. Also, a couple of players like Andre and TJ went to school in Boston.

So we would go out there and do their different tournaments, mingle with some players that they played with in college in all different towns. We all went to different colleges, so we just made a Springfield Allstar team.

Springfield still does alumni games. They find all the best players from each school in the city, and it's a highly organized event. They put it in bracket form. They do it at either Dunbar or at one of the high schools. They charge an admission fee to get in. It's a huge event.

They've been doing that now for the past couple of years.

The alumni tournaments started after I got paralyzed.

But before I was paralyzed, I played in everything else. Mostly the street ball tournaments. One was the Ben Schoolfield tournament. This tournament was started in memory of a young man who got killed by the police on Eastern Avenue.

They kept it going ever since he died in the 1990's.

I started playing in that tournament when I was sixteen. That's where I caught one of my first alley-oop dunks on somebody – an older person. It was epic.

There was a crazy crowd at Deberry park. It was about 8 o'clock at night. There was a bunch of smoke around the court. Mad drug dealers betting on the game.

One year, my cousin who was going to school in New York got an invite to the Rucker. It's one of the best basketball tournaments in the world. It's held in Harlem, New York. It's crazy.

My cousin was playing, but they were short a player. I just happened to be up there visiting. I had shorts under every pair of clothes I wore – I was always prepared to ball. So they were like, "You want to play?"

My cousin was like, "Yeah, he can ball!"

So I played. My cousin was having a terrible game. When I jumped in, I stepped up. I had twelve points off the bench, and I was playing in some sneakers that were a little too small. They were some dress sneakers. Some sneakers I just wore to chill in. But I laced up – I didn't care. When it came to ball, that's how I was. I would drop anything to go play some ball.

So I played in the Rucker. Scored twelve points.

My cousin didn't do too good.

They were talking mad shit. If you don't play good in the Rucker, those New York people are crazy. They don't play. They talk hella shit. They were like, "Get him out of here! Get him out on a Metro Platinum card. He's a bum! Where's he going – what school is he going to?"

They were talking all kinds of shit.

He had said he was going to Cincinnati, so they all knew that. They were calling him Cincinnati Boy.

I kind of salvaged the day for him. I came off the bench. Dude tried to dunk on me and I blocked him. I scored a couple buckets. Talked a little shit. The crowd goes crazy when you talk shit. They start talking with you. They are all in your face. It gets intense. But it's a dope atmosphere. I'll never forget that.

We Made History

There's another tournament called the Osgood tournament. It's in Connecticut.

We brought a team out there. We were playing against a couple of NBA players that come from CT. We made it to the finals one year, and won it. We came back the next year and made it to the finals, and won it again. We were the second team from Springfield to do that in like the last twenty years.

We're in a book. They got a little book they put out every year called the Osgood. That tournament has been going for about 40 years. It's got history. It's called the Osgood Classic Tournament.

We are written down in history out there.

A Springfield team. My Springfield team.

My stepbrother was the one who put the funds up to sponsor us to get out there. Richard Freeman. He used to do a lot of that. That was my main man. He had an extra couple of dollars.

He put it toward the team.

Chapter 5: College

A Bumpy Road

WHEN TIME CAME FOR COLLEGE, I RAN INTO a little bit of difficulty.

I was actually going to go to prep school on a partial scholarship to a school in Vermont. We couldn't afford it. At that time, there was no one else around to help me pay for it either.

I know that if a couple of my cousins, Ron and Deacon, weren't in jail, they would have paid for me to go to prep school. My cousin Ron, I grew up looking up to him. He was always smarter than other guys. He told me to stay away from all the BS, and to just play ball. If I did good in school, he agreed to make sure my feet were good. That's all I really cared about in high school and middle school – my feet.

Back to prep school: If I would have gotten to go to prep school, I'm pretty sure I would have made it professionally, for either football or basketball. Prep school sets you up for that kind of success. They also set you up really good for college.

I really wanted to go when I was accepted, because all the kids that I played AAU with in Boston went on to prep school. The really good kids went. If I lived in Boston, I would have gotten to go, because it was closer.

But even though I wasn't able to go, I made the best of what I had.

After the prep school situation, we thought about Syracuse.

They offered a full scholarship, but my grades weren't good enough.

So we went to Henry Thomas.

He was a Umass Alumnus and former athlete. He advocated for me and got me a partial scholarship to UMass starting me off on academic probation. You could only practice and lift weights. I was working out twice a day and playing football and basketball. Then school started and I felt like a home away from home. I had to learn the campus, etc.

UMass has a sports booklet that included all athletes. Because I was in the book, I was very popular already so it made it easier to transition. I was a freshman, but I was taken in by the seniors. They showed me the ropes and ways to get by in college.

He Never Got to See Me Play

You would think that with me being in college at UMass, based on my high school track record with sports, that life would be smooth sailing for me.

It wasn't.

Instead, my freshman year at UMass was one of the most difficult times in my life.

After I finally got into the school and was on my way, tragedy struck.

And it struck in a major way.

Right before Thanksgiving, around November 23rd, I got a phone call from one of my cousins.

"Mike! Come home. You gotta come home. Something happened with your dad."

I immediately went into high alert.

"What do you mean? He's good, right? Is he alright?!"

My cousin paused. "Yeah. He's alright. But we need you to come home."

I didn't know what to make of my cousin's words, but I didn't have much time to process them either. I jumped into action, borrowing one of my teammate's cars and heading to Springfield.

When I got to the hospital, something wasn't right.

I found out that my dad was in ICU.

"ICU?! I thought you said he was okay!"

But my dad was not okay.

Essentially, my family didn't want to give me this news over the phone, so they only told me enough to get me to come to the hospital. He was hooked up to the machine, but it was time to pull the plug because he was already gone.

He never got to see me play.

All through high school, my dad was locked up.

He would hear about my games, and see the newspaper clippings, but he never got to actually see me live in action.

I thought we would finally have our chance when I got to UMass.

I planned on showing out, just for him.

But due to the fact that he was stabbed to death by a person on the streets, he never got the opportunity.

What makes matters worse is that the man who killed him barely served a decade in prison before his release.

As you can imagine, I was fucked up over that.

I began a downward spiral. My motivation was lost. My drive was demolished.

I focused on having fun to try to escape the pain.

I was messing up in every way, but I didn't care anymore.

I felt like school was just not for me. I had lost too much.

How could I bounce back from this?

When The Heat Sets In

Unfortunately, my experiences of hardships didn't really let up from there.

As I said before, once my dad was killed, I was on a downward spiral.

I used sex and drugs to mask the pain.

Yes, I had fun, but a large part of me was doing what I was doing to numb my emotions.

My numbers at UMass were... astronomical.

I repressed my negative mindset and focused on having a good time. It came easily for me because of my extroverted personality.

I hurt a few girls' feelings, but I used to smooth it out. All it took was a little more loving. That's all.

At UMass, there were chicks from all around the world. It was crazy. And since my name and profile were in the book of student athletes, I was already highly sought after. I was getting love from all types of chicks in my freshman year.

I put up Wilt Chamberlain numbers. Over 100, easy. It was wicked. It was crazy.

It was my practice. Practice makes perfect.

There were a couple girls that made me kind of want to feel like I should settle down, but I couldn't. I couldn't get to that place. I couldn't grasp it. Most of the girls I dealt with knew that I wasn't interested in commitment. They didn't really care much. A lot of them would act like they cared sometimes, but that was most likely due to the fact that I was able to make them feel good. I knew how to talk to them. I knew how to treat them right, no matter the time or place. I treated every single woman with respect and I would never take anything from them.

Even though I was having a lot of fun with the ladies, things very swiftly started to take a turn for the worse, yet again.

There was one night after the club.

Everyone was rowdy and drunk.

The cops were telling everybody to leave the parking lot.

I was drunk and I jumped into the driver's seat of my boy's car. Ever confident, as the light turned yellow, I banged a left.

Red and blue. The sirens blared.

I was shitfaced.

The officer came to the window and asked, "You know why I pulled you over? Get out the car. License and registration."

I was terrified. I started to get out of the car, acting what I thought was calmly and coolly. It only took a second for me to realize that I'd forgot one critical detail: shifting out of drive.

The car started going down a hill.

I was dragging my foot. I slammed the gearshift to park, and BOOM. At first I'd thought I'd hit something...a parked car, a building, or worse. Then I realized it was the police. They threw me on the side of the car and the metal handcuffs clanged. I felt my cheek against the hood.

They were being assholes, screaming at me and acting all crazy. My friends were scared too, but they weren't really the targets – I was. I ended up being by myself because they let everyone who was riding with me go. They let someone else in the car who had their license drive it away, while they put me in the back of the cruiser.

They harassed me at the station until my boy came and bailed me out.

That was my first run in with the UMass police.

From that moment forward, it got worse and worse. I was marked, basically.

I was known by them.

Before enrolling at UMass, I didn't know I would be targeted on my own college campus. I was treated differently; I was black and I was *only* an athlete. An outsider. Racism was prevalent. It felt like every officer knew who I was and treated me accordingly.

I want to make a distinction here about my interactions with police officers.

Regardless of the fact that Amherst is just a thirty minute drive from my home, I was in a whole new world where I was the target. I had never been arrested in Springfield, where arrest rates among my peers are among the highest in the state. No record, nothing. I was a blue collared, black dude. I was loved by all Springfield people, period.

In Amherst, in the midst of the predominately white, upper-middle class academics, I felt like I had a target on my back.

You can see that once they start a trail, they make sure that they can get you any way that they can. Lesson to brothers out there: Just make sure that when you go to a college town and you know that it's a white owned or white-predominant city, you gotta watch your back.

You gotta move real smooth. Don't leave any type of trail for them to mess your life up, because they will. With no hesitation. Any means necessary. Any type of situation.

They looked for anything they could do to bring me down. You see that every day out here. And there's no way you can fight it. You got to be real with yourself, or you're going down.

Any white cop I came in contact with in Amherst did not like me.

I'm not talking about Springfield cops.

It was the UMass Amherst campus police force. They had real state troopers working there. Then they had five surrounding cities with like two cops in each city that had nothing to do.

They had nothing else to do but chase Black college kids and ruin their lives.

A few of my teammates experienced the same things. Whenever they saw us with white women, we were targeted. They did not like interracial relationships at all.

It's the exact same way today. It hasn't changed.

This has been the history for Black men in America, no matter how much our country tries to deny it and claim we've progressed. Black dudes going to jail for being accused of raping a chick because after they break up, the girl gets mad and makes up a story, or the father doesn't like him, and he makes something happen because he is connected with the cops. It happens left and right. You can't beat it. There's no way to stop it.

It's not just common – it's expected. We go through this every day. You have to know how to jump over that wall before you can get past anything.

This is one of the reasons I am writing this book. To speak to athletes that have been through a struggle, and you're doing good now, and you're trying to make something positive out of nothing. You gotta be careful.

You can't cross anybody that's of higher stature who has their hand in the law. They can reach out and touch you. They will take you right off your pedestal, quick.

They don't see you as a 17-18-year old kid – they see you as a 17-18-year-old nigger. They don't look at you as a person.

Target Practice

I felt the full force of police misconduct and racial profiling when, during my freshman year, I was falsely accused of rape.

A young woman got drunk in Springfield at the Hippodrome. She ended up getting in the car with a man she did not know. She asked him if he was me, he said yes, and he forced her to perform oral sex. Whether or not he resembled me, I do not know.

On the night of this incident, I was at a party in a dorm on campus at UMass. This was established not only by my word alone, but by the multiple eyewitnesses who recalled me throwing up in the hallway of the dorm I lived in. Another resident, a girl from my dorm, took care of me and let me crash in her room. I was in my dorm, my home away from home. I was, I felt at the time, a world away from downtown Springfield.

The allegation rocked me to my core.

I respect women.

Moreover, I thought of myself as a sex symbol already. Chicks were throwing themselves at me; I would never *take* anything. I was raised by a woman, and I had four sisters to look over. The accusation that I could commit this act and cause this type of pain was incomprehensible.

I found out about the rape allegation when the police came and kicked in the door.

I was in my boy's dorm room. We were smoking weed and playing the latest *Madden*. We thought we heard someone knocking, but we didn't think much of it.

The next thing we knew, police were blasting into the room.

We practically jumped out of our skin from the sound of them kicking in the door.

They surrounded us.

There were so many cops there, I couldn't even count them.

One of them put a bean bag gun in my face.

I almost saw my life flash before my eyes.

I thought he was going to shoot me.

They told me to put the game down. All I could see was the gun in my face. It was crazy. I was scared as fuck.

They didn't even tell me what the charges were – they just took me out in handcuffs, in front of everyone.

They harassed me, taunting me, all the way to the station.

"You're going down," they said. "You did some fucked up shit."

I had no idea what they were talking about.

When I got to the station, they finally told me that I was arrested for rape.

I couldn't believe my ears.

"You got one phone call!" They told me.

I called my grandmother's house. I was crying my eyes out.

"Mike, did you do it?"

"Grandma, you know I didn't do this!"

My aunt got on the phone. "Mike, tell me the truth: Did you do it?"

"Auntie! I would never steal anything from no girl. I was raised by women. I have four sisters! I would go crazy if something like this happened to one of my sisters."

I also tried to tell the officers that they had the wrong guy, but of course they didn't listen.

My denials fell on deaf ears.

They tried to convince my grandmother and my aunt that I did it. They didn't know...

They didn't know what to say because the police were making it seem like I did it so bad.

It took a few days for my family to contact people to get together enough bail money to post. It was $7,500, but it did not come close to securing my freedom.

Although I would never say that jail is the "place to go" or that there is any good in being incarcerated, I can say that when I was in jail, thankfully, I wasn't treated badly.

Despite the fact that I was falsely accused of rape, I was a local celebrity, so everybody loved me. They knew I didn't do it, despite what the officers said. Even the CO's treated me good. They would give me pizza, hamburgers... It was kind of a unique situation.

I also didn't have a rough time in jail because of who my dad was. He was in jail a lot. My name was ringing bells at the time because I was always in the newspaper for good stuff. Inmates read the newspaper a lot. They absolutely knew I didn't do it. Go figure.

When you go to jail for something like rape, most times, people look at you crazy. The other inmates try to fight you and beat you up, because they think you're a rapist. But everybody knew I wasn't no type of rapist. They all had my back. Everybody had my back.

When I got out, my mom and everyone just told me to keep my nose clean, and stay away from trouble. They told me I had to realize that I was a young Black man and I was targeted by situations like that.

The case was headed toward trial. I consented to DNA testing, and when the results came back, there was no match between myself and the victim. She never showed up to court. They just quaffed it. They continued without a finding.

The girl was from New Hampshire. I was told she had moved home and never heard her story.

They never found the actual guy that did it.

This ordeal was hard to get past, on top of still dealing with my father's death.

I was out there playing so hard, and I used to kill the teams. Gary Forbes, Ray Ray, I was out there just killing them. They loved me. The whole basketball team wanted me to try out with them. They wanted me to play.

My freshman year at UMass, I won the intramural championship. Me and a couple Springfield dudes. Ant Gibbs, John Fuller, Drew Rossi, a bunch of us. It was pretty dope.

Looking back, I still say I had a great freshman year, even though I went through all that.

I always try to see the positive, even in a negative situation.

The rape charge situation unfortunately tainted my image in the eyes of some of the public. Some people looked at me like I was guilty, especially in my hometown. White people would look at me funny, like I did it. They would act differently toward me sometimes just because of the way the situation was brought up. I hated it.

I'm a really good guy. I would never do anything like that. I want to make that very clear.

They Got What They Wanted

Unfortunately, that wasn't the end of my interactions with the law.

I got to sophomore year and went for a little bit, then I got kicked out mid-way through. One night, my best friend got into a fight with hockey player over a parking space. I tried to mediate and stepped in between them. Because I was Black, stronger, and bigger, I was the focal point. When someone hit the hockey player with a tire iron, it looked like it was me because you could see me. I went home to Springfield, and the next morning I was on the news. I didn't do anything but try to help the kid out after I had seen him on the floor. He was bleeding. I was the closest one to him, so I again had a target on my back.

I was charged with felony assault of the hockey player. I was sentenced, along with my friends Fola Aiyeku, Justin Etter, and Jason Becker, to be incarcerated in Northampton. That was a growing and humbling experience. It let me know I wasn't unstoppable.

When I got to jail, my best friend Jason confessed to me that he had used the tire iron. His confession was too little, too late. Jason Becker was the one who actually got into the fight and caused the injury. He didn't tell me til he got in jail. I don't know why. He just tried to be a cool white boy, because he hung out with the brothers.

My anger at Jason was overwhelming. There's no excuse for letting your innocent friends go through all that because of your actions.

Unfortunately, that still wasn't the last time I went to jail.

I was hit with a probation violation for a single dirty urine – marijuana only. It was my first violation of any terms of my probation. I felt like they were making an example out of me. Looking back, what's crazy is that I was sentenced to thirty days jail by the Northampton probation office. While I was in there, I tried to make the most of my time by playing one-on-one basketball games in the Rec Deck. I never lost a game – even against Kevin Crapps, who was one of the best guys in there. I beat him multiple times.

So I made the most out of what could have been a depressing situation. Ironically, today, that office is located less than a mile from one of the largest marijuana dispensaries in the state.

Running From The Law

I never did anything to actually force a cop's hand.

But leave it to them, and I'm a piece of shit.

Plus, when you are accused of rape, they look at you wrong, no matter what. Especially white cops. That always was in the back of my head. That made me stay away a little bit, and made me travel more.

An epic moment happened during my winter break at UMass, however.

One of my best friends was going to school in Burlington, Vermont. I went up there to chill with him. He played for the basketball team at Saint Michaels. During the break, athletes usually stay on campus. It was the girl's basketball team, the boy's basketball team, the hockey team, and a couple of other teams that stayed up there.

My white friend, Ryan Maloney wasn't too big. He was a little scrawny white boy. He was a real humble, cool dude. Not a troublemaker or anything. So we were up there chilling with him. I was actually at a party with the girl's basketball team. I was chilling. I was drunk. We were having a good time.

All of a sudden, one of my boys came and said, "Yo, they're messing with Ryan. They're trying to jump him."

It was Andy Owens – he came with me. He was frantic. I just blacked out.

I did a 40-yard dash across a football field. I slid on the ice and fell on my face. I jumped up and kept running. I was pissed that they were messing with my boy.

I got to the dorm room, and there were at least 12 dudes lined up in the dorm hallway. They were standing across from each other, side to side. I went down the hallway, knocking them all out one by one. BOOM! BOOM! I was knocking them out.

I got to the end where Ryan was at. There was a guy there bothering him.

I went HAM. I knocked him out.

All of a sudden, a security guard came and said, "Hey! Who are you? What's your name?"

I got scared and started running.

I got off of campus and onto a main road.

All of a sudden, I saw a cop car coming. There was a pile of snow. I dived into the pile of snow to try to hide from the cop. The car went by and I got up. I went to the nearest gas station. The cop came back.

He said, "Were you just on a college campus? Come with me."

They took me down. I got arrested. They were being assholes.

I had to go to court the next morning.

The judge was like, "So, there was a fight last night at the college campus. There were twelve hockey players against one basketball player? Aren't hockey players supposed to be tough? Donate $100 to any charity in Vermont, and you're all set."

I said, "Okay. The police ain't too bad out here!"

Extra-Curriculars

I'm a multi-dimensional dude.

As I said before, my mom really instilled hustling in my blood. She's a stone cold hustler. She did everything for herself since she was thirteen. Her and my grandma had their differences so she left the house early and she just survived on her own.

I could apply hustling to sports, school, or whatever I was doing.

She taught me to hustle hard.

I been selling weed my whole life. No one would really know that because I never really put it out in the open, but I sold weed. It's legal now. I'm not saying I do it anymore, but I hustled all through high school.

My mom and dad both hustled.

They called my dad Break Em Down. That meant that he could take the littlest thing and break it down and make more money off of it than regular people. I definitely picked up that trait. Everybody his age would call me Lil Break Em Down.

I took that to the basketball court, breaking people down and scoring easy.

I also broke down weed and sold it easy, and sold it for more.

When I first got to college, I wasn't really a drinker. I was more just a weed smoker. I smoked weed a lot. I been smoking weed since about sophomore year of high school. Weed used to help me calm down. It was like medicine.

I used to smoke sometimes before games. I was a high adrenaline guy, so weed used to help me calm down and see everything a lot clearer. I really think weed helped me get through high school and college. I didn't smoke it to overwhelm myself. I used it like a Ritalin, or like a drug that would amp me up the right way, slow down my thought process, and help me see a lot clearer.

My intuition is amazing when it comes to sports. I see stuff before it happens. That was my gift – being able to seek something out before it's actually about to be done. That was pretty dope. College coaches and the pros look for that. So they definitely said I was a pro in high school because of the way I played.

And I owe it all to the weed.

When I was in high school, college… At UMass, I met all types of dudes out there that grew weed. Weed connoisseurs. Weed was just in my life. It always was.

Once I got introduced to it, it was a wrap. I just took that and ran with it.

There have been mad crazy situations with it.

Taking it from white boys – little scrawny dudes who had too much. Weed was so big at UMass. It was like another world. I was introduced to some hippies. They were showing me the different ways and how weed is vital to life and just the ins and outs of it. I just fell in love with it. It's always been a part of my life.

Now that dispensaries are opening, I was thinking about trying to see if we can open a dispensary out here. They have them in Northampton and Pittsfield, Easthampton... they're popping up all over the place. But they don't have one directly in Springfield yet.

They are trying. There are like five sites right now that are trying.

There should be one opening very soon.

That's the new way to try to stop the black market. But you never can stop the black market. It's just going to inflate the prices. The black market will just have to go back to the 2001 and 2002 prices.

That weed talk is really my lane. It's always been in my life.

I'm a weed connoisseur.

I did have a few scandalous moments during my weed dealing career.

One time at UMass, some dude came from Vermont with some big backpacks full of bud. He came to my boy's crib. My boy had already told me, like "Mike, I want you to just take this shit. Just take it."

I was like, "You sure?" You know me – I wasn't scared of anything.

I had a dude who walked him upstairs. He laid a couple of pounds out on the bed. We were talking about it. My boy gave me the head nod.

I started picking up all the pounds. These things are like pillow cases. I stuff them in the bag.

I'm talking to him all nonchalant.

He's still talking – I don't think he even picked up that I'm about to do something.

We were supposed to be buying it from him.

I grabbed the whole two backpacks, and he was such a little scrawny kid. I ran out of the room and I held the door so he couldn't open it. I did it for about ten seconds. He just – I know he was trying his fucking hardest to open this door.

There were about twenty steps.

I jumped straight down the twenty steps, and there was a window in the living room that was open. I dove through the window, and my other boy was outside waiting for me. I jumped right in the van and came all the way back to Springfield.

And that was it.

When it came to taking weed and stuff like that, I never did any of that to anyone from Springfield. I never did it to people I knew or grew up with. I made sure nothing bad came across my path. I wouldn't do no dirt in my hometown or nothing like that. I'm loyal to my people.

But as for scrawny Vermont kids who have endless amounts of weed at their house because they grow it, it was fair game. The kid I robbed had an endless supply that he grew at his house. These kids were hippies. These kids were chemists. These dudes got whole farms. They're living good because it's all free. Their parents have been doing it for years. It's passed down to them.

They wanted to charge us $3,000 a pound. I was like, "Man… Yeah, I'll see you later."

I did the dash with it all the way back to Springfield. Took care of my people, made a couple dollars. Then I went right back to school like nothing happened.

All in a day's work.

There were a few times I almost got caught with weed in my possession.

One time we were at a Wu Tang and Busta Rhymes concert at UMass. They came and performed. Me and my boys rolled like ten L's each. We didn't know if you could or couldn't. Busta Rhymes and all them were on stage smoking.

They were saying, "Whoever got L's, roll up your spliffs!"

So we were on top looking down at the bottom. We rolled up and started smoking. The security came out of nowhere. We had a pound in the bag. Boom. We all went to the security room. But it wasn't that big of a deal. We were all athletes so they let it slide.

That was one of my scary moments in college.

I'm still the weed man to this day.

Setbacks

After I got out I went back to UMass. They lifted the trespassing warrant they had for me. It wasn't working out. I went for a year then came back to Springfield. Lived with my mom.

The Amherst people had something against me because I was from Springfield. When you go to Amherst, they put a tag on you. He's a local Black kid. Athlete.

They don't think too highly of you, the police out there.

I went through all those years being built up in my community with tons of support from all around, only to get to college and be targeted because of the color of my skin and where I was from. They change your whole life with little situations. They dictate your life for you. And there's nothing you can do about it. Once you're in that system, you're in their hands, and they just toy with you.

I swear, it's like they played with my life. After they had the little rape situation, they tried to get me on whatever they could.

I didn't finish my career at UMass, but I did go back. I tried to, but the way they look at you on campus kind of makes you feel like an asshole. You kind of shy away from people, because it puts you into a type of depression. I bounced back from it fairly fast though. I wasn't going to let it hold me down. I was too big for that shit.

Chapter 6: Continued Education

AIC/STCC

AFTER UMASS, I WENT TO AIC FOR roughly a year and a half, basically two.

The first semester, I was doing really good. My grades were up. But then I violated probation right at the end of the semester when I was going to be eligible to play for the football team and basketball team.

So it screwed me up.

Then I gave it another try.

I went to STCC, got my grades up at STCC and transferred back to AIC. So I wasn't giving up.

That's one thing I could tell kids: If you get opportunities, take advantage of your opportunities. Life is only but so long, and you never know what's going to happen.

I used to try to take advantage of whatever opportunities were afforded to me. Help I got from any teachers, professors, presidents, whoever. The mayor even loves me around Springfield. They always try to help, and I take it. I take advantage of it.

I ended up going to jail from AIC for violating the probation. I was in there for four months. But it wasn't bad, you know what I mean? When you got a name in Springfield and you go to jail, they kind of treat you really good. Especially if it's about sports.

All the CO's are former athletes, usually, so you get little perks. Like pizza, burgers, little treats that regular people just don't get.

Nobody tried to come at me sideways at all. That was never going to happen. My dad was in jail for basically my whole life so he solidified... I was good.

When I got out of jail, I wanted to get back in school, but I had too much going on.

AIC had given me a partial scholarship. Once I went to jail, I lost the scholarship. They took it from me. That was what ended my career at AIC.

I couldn't afford to stay.

I loved AIC. AIC is amazing, because it's an American International College, and it really was international beauty. There were so many beautiful women from all over. I had an amazing time with the women there. They loved me, and I loved them.

I put up pretty good numbers there too, but me being from Springfield, it's my hometown so I was a king on campus. All the people from every other place, whenever they would be off campus they could just ask my name, and people would be like, "Oh my God – you really know everyone in Springfield!"

They used to think I was bragging and boasting about how much my name was good in Springfield. I told them that whenever they needed something – it could go from drugs to anything legal – if it's moving around, I know everyone, or I know who to get in touch with.

I have connections with people who do promotions for clubs, parties, getting in places… I can get people in anywhere downtown. That's how good my name was. Just being a good guy and a cool dude. Everything was just perfect. That's why I love my city so much.

Everyone treated me good. They treated me like royalty.

And I took advantage of everything I could at the time.

Friends After UMass

One of my best friends I met after leaving UMass was Nick Clement. Just like the Maloney's, the Clement family and I also hit it off from the start.

I met Nick through my cousin Andre. They were going to school at Brandeis. I used to chill with Andre and TJ, then I started hanging with Nick.

He introduced me to a lot of people, including his friends from Belchertown and Granby. When Nick would come home, we hung out from Thursday through Sunday, just having fun. We're both die hard Eagle's fans, and his family are season ticket holders. They took me to some of the games with them. It was epic.

Nick and I also had some crazy nights.

One time we went to an Eagles game. We were in Philly. After the game we were hanging out with his aunts. His aunts are mad cool. They were older but they didn't mind chilling with us.

Later that evening, Nick and I headed to a strip club.

When we got inside, we immediately noticed that things looked a little different. We were split up, so he went in one room and I went in another.

In the room I went to, there was a girl behind a glass.

I said, "What the hell is this?!"

They gave me some hand lotion and some napkins and said, "Enjoy."

I was like, "Man, I don't want this shit!"

I kicked my way through the door. I said, "Get me out of here!"

Nick was in another room and they had him surrounded.

There was some big dude trying to take Nick's money. I kicked through the door.

I said, "Give him his fuckin money back!"

The dude was scared of me, so he gave him the money back. I smacked the other dude. I kicked the door open and me and Nick ran up out of there.

That was one of the craziest night ever.

Semi-Pros

Another thing I continued for a while after college was football.

I ended up playing a lot of semi pro. My cousin's team – Eric Brown – I used to play for him. He had two teams. The Blitzin Bears and The Warriors.

I played semi pro for about three to four years off and on.

One year with the Warriors, I won the national championship. This was right before I got shot. I have a ring for that. I have four rings total.

I also played one year of arena football with the New England Surge.

The semi pro team is who got me the invite from them. I played for the Blitzen Bears and they got me the invite.

We had a nice, successful season. I got paid $300 a game, plus perks. We lived at the Sheraton Hotel in Worcester, down by the DCU Center. We used to terrorize the city. We would eat all the food we could at the hotel and charge it to the team. At the end of the year, the coach called us all together for a meeting and he was so mad because he had to pay the whole bill.

We ended up having a good season, but at the end of the season, the team went bankrupt. That's what made us stop. Our stay at the Sheraton was all inclusive. The cost for thirty players was quite a lot. We were ordering steaks every night, lobster... I took full advantage of it.

I was like, "Man, I don't eat like this on a regular basis. I'm ordering everything!" I ordered extra pillows, extra covers... everything was charged to the room. I was ordering Pay Per View, nasty night... all that. I took full advantage. He said it was free, so I said, "Man. I'm charging it to the game!"

And I guess it caught up to us.

But we had a good time that year.

After that team went bankrupt, I wasn't really able to go with another team. That one was the closest one in the area. There were a couple of other teams, like one in New York, and there was one I was going to try out for in Texas called the Dallas Desperados. I got an invite to their team, but I never really got to go do it.

But it was fun while it lasted.

Everything started getting darker when I wasn't doing much. I was just hustling, honestly, trying to make ends meet.

I just stopped playing football after a while.

The semi pros aren't bad if you are young and you have time and there is a good team in your area. If you have all that, you should definitely play. It's a stepping stone. It will help you get stronger and better. Sometimes if it's a good league, you can get seen and get invited to other opportunities like arena teams, or Canadian football teams.

There's a lot of opportunities out there.

I did have some scandalous moments when I played semi pro as well.

There was an all-star game that I played in that all the semi pro players get to go play in. It was in Vegas. That was an amazing time. It was an all-inclusive trip, for three days and four nights.

We went down there, and we went out one night, and we met some dudes who thought we were professional football players. They were like, "You guys are hanging with us for the night!" These were some rich ass white dudes. They just kept us with them all night through VIPs, telling everybody we bumped into, "These are professional football players!" They were giving us names. We just went along with it. Then when we went to this one club, we bumped into a bridal shower.

It was a bunch of nurse practitioners.

One of the chicks was like, in love with me. So I went back to the room with her. We were getting it in. We were mad loud. She was making mad noises. All of a sudden, we get a knock at the door. It was the friend that was getting married's parents.

They were like, "We can hear everything you guys are saying!"

The girl that was getting married came, and she was going crazy on the chick I was with. She was screaming at her. So the chick I was with ended up getting a hotel room for us at a whole other hotel. She felt so embarrassed.

She left me with the room for the whole night.

Fun times.

Chapter 7: When Darkness Rose

I Met a Girl…

MY LIFE WAS STILL ON A DOWNWARD SPIRAL, but I didn't really notice it.

Then things took the worst possible turn they could take.

I met this girl, and she had a baby father that was an alcoholic and drug addict. I didn't know it at the time.

One night, he actually was creeping around the crib, and I saw him. That was actually God trying to tell me I shouldn't be in that place. But me being me, I was like, "Man, whatever. I can handle myself."

Another night, I saw him walking around the crib again, drunk. I was like, "What are you doing around here?" He had called her phone earlier and said, "I want the W2's for my kids. Those are my kids. I'm filing taxes this year."

I was like, "Man, this dude is a weirdo." Like… all of a sudden, he was calling the phone, like crazy. One day I saw her phone and saw that she had like 12 missed calls from her baby daddy. You would think I would have started to put two and two together.

But I didn't understand the extent of his mental instability until it was too late.

Tragedy Strikes

It was February 8th – my father's birthday. He had passed away 10 years prior.

I was drinking and reminiscing about the times we had shared. At around 11:00 or 12:00 o'clock, I decided to go lie down. My girlfriend at the time was already in bed. Her three children had been asleep for hours. I heard a loud noise in the back of the house.

Immediately, I felt a chill down my spine.

Something wasn't right.

What I heard had sounded like a gunshot.

I went downstairs to see what was going on.

When my foot hit the bottom step, I heard somebody coming.

I went back upstairs and hid the oldest child in a closet, along with his twin siblings, who were infants at the time. I made sure that they were safe, then went back to the staircase to face the intruder.

From the top of the steps, I saw my girlfriend's ex-boyfriend, the father of their children, standing at the bottom.

I asked him, "What are you doing here?"

He looked up at me and said, "I came here to kill myself."

I tried to redirect him.

"Brother, you shouldn't even be here. What's going on with you?"

He started to approach, bounding up the steps two at a time.

Adrenaline began coursing through my veins. I knew right away that it was about to be on. As soon as his foot hit the top step, we were fighting. I got the best of him. He fell down the steps and I heard something loud fall out of his pocket.

It sounded like metal, and I knew it was the gun.

I heard him cock the hammer back.

Time froze.

Somehow I got inside the room and tried to shut the door. He shot through it. It made me back up. When I backed up, BOOM. Another shot hit me in my right arm. The door opened and he stood behind it. He still had the gun in his hands.

I didn't have time to think about pain.

My autonomic system was in overdrive as I launched myself at him.

We began tussling for the gun...

I'm fighting with one hand.

I kind of push him away.

I started running.

I turn around and I see my only exit. I dove straight through the glass window. He's shooting at me as I go out the window.

I hit the ground, and he kept shooting. He shot me in the back. I could not move. The EMT's took about fifteen to twenty minutes to arrive.

The next door neighbor came outside. I heard her talking to me as I was kind of fading. The words "just hold on" are seared in my memory. It was a blur until I finally saw the EMT's.

I remember thinking one female EMT was beautiful. And then everything went black. I woke up in the hospital a week later with a million people outside trying to make sure I was good.

I was told that the shooter went into the other room, shot and killed my girlfriend, and then killed himself. It was a triple shooting. A homicide. And a suicide.

The children lost their mother and their father that night. They are now with their grandparents.

I see them once in a while because I keep in touch with her cousin. She brought them by to see me last year. They're doing good. They are getting bigger and bigger. They're five now.

They really have no recollection of what happened because they are so young. I keep in touch with them as they get older. I will explain to them one day how good their mom was.

It's deep.

You're Never Gonna Walk Again

I was out for almost a week before I came back to.

My body and mind were struggling in ICU. I was fighting for my life.

When I woke up in the hospital, I was shocked.

I kind of remembered what happened. I was thinking, "Oh, I'll be alright. This is just one of those phases you go through."

But then everything sets in and reality hits. I couldn't even use my arms. All I could move was my head and my neck. It was tough. Then they had me on a tracheotomy.

After being shot and going to the hospital, I couldn't speak. It was crazy trying to communicate with everybody. I was coughing up my phlegm.

I was in Baystate first. Then they shipped me right from Baystate to Boston. Right to physical therapy at Spalding. Probably one of the best physical therapy facilities you could go to in the east coast. I was out there for a full year, and then insurance started telling me that I had no more time. They sent me home. When they do that, you have to deal with wherever you are at.

Western Mass has the worst physical therapy. There aren't really any up to date therapy programs out here. So, you gotta basically try to do it yourself. You gotta stay in tune with life and not let it swallow you up.

I have PTSD from that night. I don't really suffer from flashbacks too much, but loud noises really mess me up. The 4th of July... I'm all set with that.

When it first happened, I couldn't be by myself. I did not like being alone at all. It already sucks not being able to do anything for yourself. But then when no one is around, it's like, the walls are suffocating and falling in on you. It kind of throws you for a loop.

When it comes to being paralyzed, there are a lot of things people take for granted. They don't realize many things we have to have done for us. For example, I can't expel my own feces. You have to have somebody dig into your body and take out your feces.

That's a hard situation. You don't want anybody random doing that to you. One time, they tried to have a guy do it when I was in the hospital. I was like, "What the hell is wrong with y'all? I don't want no dude digging up my ass to get nothing. I don't care who it is. If he's that happy to do it, that means something ain't right with him. You not about to have me doing that."

That's just one thing.

Another thing is, when you are eating, it's like... you don't want anything.

Your mouth... I see why women who suffer from bulimia and anorexia tend to hide food in their mouths. I used to do that. I used to act like I ate, but I would have a chunk of food in my mouth. You can't eat. Your body rejects it for a while. It won't let you eat.

Plus, you're taking mad pain pills, and the pain pills just make you skinnier and skinnier because you are not eating. You're just taking pain pills and drinking juice and water. That takes a toll on your body. It sets you back. If you don't battle through that, you're a goner. You can die, because if all you are doing is taking the pain pills, you are not gaining any weight. It begins to eat away at your body.

One of the hardest conversations I ever had was the conference with the doctor.

Realizing that I wasn't walking and that I wasn't about to be able to get right back up, being an athlete...

When we had the doctor conference, the doctor walked in – he was an arrogant asshole. He was like, "So... You'll probably never walk again. You'll probably just be able to move your head. It's highly unlikely that you'll be able to do anything else."

I looked at him and looked at Nicole and my mom. I was like, "Yeah, aight. You got the wrong one."

He had just walked in and said that.

It was kind of intense.

A tear dropped from my eye, but me being myself, I already knew like, it was time to fight. It was time to figure something out.

When It Rains, It Pours

After I had to be transferred to the Western Mass physical therapy when the insurance stopped paying in Boston, I went into a depression. One thing that I learned was that if you let the injury swallow you up, you go into a deep depression. I was depressed for over two years. I was losing weight.

I got into a slump and felt like no one cared.

I kept thinking, *Where is everyone??*

When I was in Boston at Spalding, everyone came to visit me.

When I was transferred back to Springfield, it seemed like all the visits stopped.

A year after me getting shot, my little cousin, Dwayne Borbua, got into a car accident and died. He was drinking and driving. He crashed on Saint James Ave. That really hurt me. He was more like a little brother than a little cousin. I helped raise him. That was my Auntie Sheila's son. Her only son. It hurt the family too, because he was a good kid. He wasn't a troublemaker, he wasn't in or out of jail or anything… He was making moves and doing better than a lot of people older than him. He was light years ahead of his time.

I loved him. We called him D-Wade. He was like my little brother. I remember when I was dating this one chick, and he was fifteen at the time. No license, but I taught him how to drive when we were younger. I used to give him my car, and tell him to ride with me to Boston. I let him drop me and my girl off in Boston, and I would let him take the car for the weekend. I would make him come pick me back up on Monday.

He was doing that for a year and never got caught or in trouble. He was a smooth little character. I miss the hell out of him. He was always around. He always was there; that's why I loved him so much. He liked to learn from me. Me and him were really tight.

That's why when he passed, it set me into a depression. A year after my injury, he died.

Right after that, my step brother, Little Richard – Richard Freeman - got shot in the face. He is completely blind now. That happened that same year. That made me fall even deeper.

Richard's father, Big Rich, used to date my mother. He did a lot for me. He loved me, and he wanted me to be a positive role model for his son, Little Richard, who was getting into a lot of trouble. Little Richard had been sent to live with family in Atlanta for a few years to help straighten out his behavioral issues.

Big Rich sent for him to come back to Springfield so we could be together.

Around that time, he was getting sick – he had throat cancer.

But before he passed away, he made sure that me and Little Richard had a strong bond.

As I previously mentioned, Little Richard was one of my best buddies all through high school. We played football and basketball together. We were very close. The rest of his family also treated me like I was one of their own.

So you can only imagine how I felt when I found out that he too had gotten shot.

Imagine that – you just got shot, then your cousin dies, then your step brother gets shot in the face. Now he's 100% blind. But he's out here still battling back at it. We keep in touch. He's one of my right hand men too.

I Almost Lost My Life - Again

On top of those tragedies, I also had more near death experiences.

One day me and my girl, my uncle, and my brother were all at my house. My boy walked in and out of the house. He had his daughter in his hand. He walked close to the door.

All of a sudden, he panicked.

Then, we heard a bunch of bullets coming through the house from everywhere. From all angles. I'm laying in the bed. I can't move. The bullets are whistling by my face.

It was crazy.

That's one of the scariest situations since I've been paralyzed that I've been in.

That happened twice, all around the same time period.

We knew who did it, and it got taken care of. God took care of it. The person that did it is no longer here. I'm protected by God. I really know that.

Another near-death experience that God spared me from was when I had bed sores.

I was in and out of the hospital all the time.

I had the bed sores because of the open wounds in my body. I was trying not to succumb to them. I didn't have the proper bed, so I was in danger – more so than I even knew.

Long story short, one of the bed sores got so bad that the blood started to smell.

It smelled like a dead body.

I was taken to the hospital, where I was later told that if I had not gone that day, I would have died.

They gave me a blood transfusion. I coded twice.

They brought me back both times, thank God.

The infection traveled to my bones, so I had to get surgery.

It was super scary.

But thank God, I made it. And as of the time of this writing, it's been three years since my last bed sore.

Friends and Enemies, Sometimes Both

I spoke about having a strong, close-knit family. But sometimes, family can be the worst enemy. I take it with a grain of salt.

I'm a strong, smart guy, so you can't pull one over on me. It's hard to get one past me. I'm very alert. I keep my nose in everything. I'm a very observant man.

I had some family members and best friends that ended up going with my ex-girlfriends. A former friend is engaged to one of my ex-girlfriends, and a family member married one of my other ex-girlfriends. I guess I was a role model in a lot of different aspects of life. I showed people the way to live life, so to speak, or to have life live with you. All of my ex-girlfriends used to take care of me really good. I never used them or anything, but they took care of me. I'm a loving guy, so when people love me, they love me a lot. The families fall in love with me. All my exes families loved me.

One of my exes, her dad had his own painting company. He wanted me to be his apprentice. He was grooming me. He fell in love with me. He used to teach me how to paint, how to go to the auctions for housing... he used to walk me through things. That was dope. He gave me a car to make sure I could get back and forth to work and to her town where they lived so we could meet up. He bought her a new one and gave me her car. It was an Acura TL. I was part of the family.

I've had people take me on trips out of the country, get me stamps on my passport...

So I know I showed people the way. Former best friends... my former best friend is engaged to that girl whose father did all that for me.

When we talked about it, he tried to put it on me like, "Are you mad, Bro?"

I said, "Nah, Brother. I guess I showed you the way; how to do it."

What really had me baffled was that I was wondering when it started. I found out about their relationship when I saw them posting stuff on Facebook.

They were in motel rooms.

I used to go to hotels with her.

I saw a video of them on Facebook. They were making videos saying, "Are you mad, Bro?" They were trying to egg me on.

I'm like, "Brother, I don't care! You're doing stuff I already did." I showed you the fruits of the labor.

We were still friends at the time, and he randomly did this.

Once I got shot, he kind of tried to apologize, but once you cross that line, there's really no coming back from that.

That's corny. It makes you look like, what else would you do?

He's already done a lot of weird stuff toward me anyway, so I was already on my way out the door with this dude.

One of my cousins did me the same way. He just married one of my ex-girlfriends from high school. We were really close. She was in with my family. She was really close with my mom. They didn't say anything for the two years that they were dating.

I wouldn't have been mad if my cousin had just come and told me. That was a high school girlfriend, so I would have understood. He still hasn't even come to me as a man to mend it up. I made it my business to send them a congratulations on Facebook.

I said, "Whenever you feel like being a man, come talk to me. It's cool, Brother. I'm here. I'm not going to change. I love you, Bro."

When his dad died, I was there for him. My mom was there for him. That's what made me mad. He didn't even invite my mom to the wedding. She really took that personal, but it's all good. I still love my little cousin. I don't care about that stuff.

I believe he will come around one day. It takes a while.

I Almost Gave Up

During my two-and-a-half year period of depression, things got really dark. I was a shell of who I used to be due to all the weight loss and malnutrition. Losing my cousin and hearing about my stepbrother really started messing with me, along with trying to process the fact that I was told I would never walk again.

When you go through something like what I went through, you see who your friends really are. All the little stuff comes to light. You can see a lot of stuff more clearly.

I reflected a lot about what I should have done better.

I always think about different stuff I could have done, and how I could have approached it, but this is all in God's hands. Everything's already written down. I can't say it would have went any other way than the way it went. I'm just happy I made it out alive period.

And I saved some lives in the process.

During my depression, my emotions went wickedly crazy like a rollercoaster. They were hard to control. At one point, things got so bad that I started becoming delusional and hallucinating. I was biting my nails to the point where I would start to bleed. I would think that I was at various locations, but the whole time I was in the same hospital bed.

I was lashing out at my aunt, and spitting at my grandmother.

During that time, I had a UTI, and my family was trying to get me some treatment, but I was convinced that they were really trying to take me to a nursing home because no one wanted to take care of me.

I was out of my mind.

The doctors later told us they suspected that the UTI had gotten into my bloodstream and caused a chemical imbalance. That coupled with the fact that they basically accidentally gave me too many pain meds may have sparked my delusions and hallucinations.

It was a crazy time.

But when you're strong, you just tell yourself that you can make it. And I have a strong family, so they were all right there. Plus Springfield had my back. The city showed nothing but love.

But during the second year, while I was going through my depression, I was taking more and more medication and just smoking my head away.

I just didn't want to think about anything else.

I was in a fog.

If you look at any of my old photos, or any interviews on the internet, you will see how skinny I was. How malnourished I was.

I sometimes found myself basically just waiting to die.

Chapter 8: Genesis: The Rebirth

I Could See God's Hand

I ALMOST HIT ROCK BOTTOM.

I was hallucinating sometimes. I was going against my family.

Then all of a sudden, God took over my life.

My sister was heavy into church, and she just had me praying more and doing more things with God, just asking Him and seeking Him, then boom! He just took over.

Ever since then, I've been amazing.

My sister had been gradually trying to get to me. She lived in Atlanta. She just came back one day and said, "I'm not leaving my brother til he's back right."

This is the oldest girl of my siblings – Michelle.

She's one of the main reasons I'm still here and mentally sane.

She stopped everything she was doing, and came back for big bro.

God made it happen. Period.

There was nothing else to be said. She saw me in distress. She came and made it happen. She stayed with me til I was back right, for like a couple of months.

So I definitely owe a lot to her.

Every night. She stayed with me, prayed with me, breaking through different barriers. Mental barriers.

Once I got through, it was a wrap. God is good.

God was in my life. I was strong. I was ready to do whatever it was that He wanted me to do.

A turning point for me that helped me to keep on going was when I got baptized.

I gave my life to Him.

It changed my life.

God is stronger than anything. God helped my mom stop with her addiction, so I knew He would be able to help get me right. Before you knew it, I was already back to normal. I was back to myself. I was filling up – my face, my body, my neck...

I had a total before and after transformation.

During my depression I looked like a skeleton. It was crazy. The bounce back was real. I owe it all to God. God is almighty. I knew once I gave my life to Him, He was going to turn it around, so that's what I did – I went and got baptized and boom, life changed from then on. Now I'm looking good and feeling good, and everything else is rolling.

I had some counseling that was assigned to me. It helped a little bit, but it was more of me talking to my friends and family that got me through, and God.

The only counselor I needed was God.

With His help, all else is just going to have to work, because He is going to make it work.

God is straight cut and dry.
You ask for forgiveness, and you gonna get it.

Chapter 9: Where I Am Now

The Youth

I FEEL LIKE MY MAIN PURPOSE RIGHT NOW is to speak to kids.

And to let everybody know that you can get past certain crazy situations in life. I'm a walking testimony. I'm a rolling testimony.

I want to motivate and to show people that life isn't over when you are in a position where you are very vulnerable. When you are at your lowest, it is possible to bounce back.

My message to kids who are paralyzed like me is this: You are lucky.
We live in a time where every day, something is being created to make life easier for paraplegics or quadriplegics. Keep your head up. Pray. God is making a way. I want kids to stay big on God and to let them know that He is the reason I am in such a great state of mind today. God.

As far as my involvement in the community: I want to do more, but I have already talked to a couple of different schools. They played my documentary that I have for all the local high school athletes in 2018. They got to see the documentary that my boy Yousef Abdu Ali made for me.

I felt like that touched a lot of kids and let them know how my life is, how my life was growing up, and how much sports was a big opportunity and a big part of my life.

I wasn't able to go to the schools when they showed the documentary, but that is something I am interested in. I'm hoping with this book that I will be able to do that a lot.

I really want to talk to the youth.

That's why God brought me back, to talk to the youth. In any way I can, I want to help them think positively about how to prosper in life with sports.

I'm a Rolling Testimony

Being paralyzed has taught me patience and humility. It humbled me in a lot of ways.

It's a reality check.

Before my injury, I was running a thousand miles a minute, but now, I am able to slow down and see the big picture.

It's a blessing.

Most would think that you can't live a fulfilling life after what I went through, but I am here to say that that couldn't be further from the truth. You just have to find the joy.

Find what you like, and stick to that.

Appreciate the little things.

Change the way you view things – look at it from a different angle.

I learned that I could enjoy just watching a game of basketball, and telling the kids around me what I know about the game. The information I learned through my experiences is valuable. I still have a place in this world.

My message to adults with disabilities is this: You have to put God first.

Then remember that there are things that you can do.

Capture the things that you like.

I don't mind telling my story, getting into detail about being shot. I've never been shy. I'm trying to take this situation head on.

If you feel like you are down, you have to think about the world in a general sense. There is definitely someone out there in a worse position than you that needs help.

When you do get help, you have to take advantage of it. Don't just let stuff pass by. Don't be too big headed or angry about your position. You have to come to a sense with yourself like, nothing ever happens without God knowing.

So this already has been written down in His book for years. So just think about that and you can get past whatever.

You have to push forward. Your life is not over.

These are the things you shouldn't do, and these are the things you should possibly do to get to that next level. I'm really trying to be a source of inspiration, especially in my city. We don't really have any crazy really good role models besides Travis Best as far as sports.

I want to be that guy that opens up his own recreational center for kids so that they have another outlet, because we only have so many resources. Boys and Girls Club. Martin Luther King, Family Center, YMCA... that's pretty much it.

I want to have a Mike Vaz center. I want to have a roller skating rink for the kids as well as a recreational center. I want to have things for the grown-ups too. Try to bring back some entertainment around here, so everybody won't have to worry about who is shooting who, or whatever. I want us to have things to do so it's not so dead anymore.

If I would have been able to continue the physical therapy, I believe it would have definitely helped me to be in a better position than I am in now. I am most definitely trying to go back.

I am doing everything in my power to make sure I have enough money to put myself... or just hire a real physical therapist that will just come and work me out every single day. That's all it takes, is money. Money talks.

I just gotta buckle down, get a couple dollars, stack it up, and get right.

I'm definitely trying to prove all the critics wrong. Everybody that said I couldn't do it. It's possible.

Anything is possible with God. I'm a God-fearing man. I know that with Him anything is possible. I just gotta put Him first and have faith. I got all that. I got baptized three years ago. I've been changing my life. Everything has been good.

It's hard to get recognition for stories like mine when you come from a little town like Springfield. But hopefully with this book, I will be able to do everything I need to do.

My Current Support Systems

One other person that I want to mention before my story closes is my Uncle Bruce. I give him a lot of credit for just coming in and helping me out now. Even when I was walking, he would clean my room whenever I had girls coming over. I could always call him. Now with me being paralyzed, he's like my butler. I call him my butler. He does everything for me. He washes all my clothes and keeps my house clean.

He's on my dad's side. He's related to me through marriage. He's a genuine guy. He does everything straight from the heart. You really can't find good help nowadays. Everybody wants the money, but no one will do it from their heart or because they love you.

Being the person I was, I always helped and gave out money when I had it. That's what separates me from a lot of people. I believe that's one of the reasons I am shown so much love now. I was a genuine dude. I'm one of a kind. I don't change. I don't act different to anybody, and I can blend in or fit in anywhere. Any type of situation, I can adapt to it. That's one of my main traits.

Uncle Bruce is a good dude. He does a lot for me. He deals with my attitude, my ups and downs... Being in this position, there's nothing you can do but talk shit because that's all you got. I talk my shit, and he deals with it.

He says, "Get it off; I know you are probably going to apologize later for being an asshole."

But it is what it is. We go through our ups and downs. In the end, he still got my back before anybody. He hasn't changed.

I've had a couple of workers who have worked for me and as soon as they got that first nice paycheck, they were gone.

I'm like, "Wow. I'm glad I helped you get your rent, but it's all good. Everything works out in the end."

I've ran through a lot of different workers so far. The shooting happened in 2013. It's been six years.

My mom has always been here, and my sisters have always been here. My brother helps out. My stepbrother helps out. It was really a family affair. I try to keep it in the family.

My Former Greatest Fear

My greatest fear used to be the thought of being left alone.

Now, I'm content being home by myself. I used to be like, "Who's going to change the channel?
What am I going to do if I need something?
Who's going to answer my phone?"

Now I can let the phone ring. The TV can be off.
I can close my eyes and take a nap.
Once you get comfortable back in your own skin, it's a big thing.
I don't need someone to be here at all times. I was babied and spoiled in the beginning, but now I feel more self-sufficient.
That was a major step for me. I was able to overcome my vulnerabilities.
You have to be willing to make that step.
You have to get to the point where you realize what happened to you. You get past the 'what ifs' and the 'what I should haves'.

Once you get past that, you are good to go.

Where I am With my Injury

I'm a C-6 Incomplete injury. This means that my spine was not completely broken. That's a good thing. I have a chance to walk again. The way I am with my life, I know I'm going to walk again. My story is not over. It's still going. I believe in the next three to four years I could be walking again with the right help.

I'm in therapy now, but it's not the same as the type of therapy I was receiving when I was first injured. There are no good machines. There's this thing called the FES bike. It puts your feet on pedals and it continuously moves just to get the blood circulating in my legs more. They also have one where you can move both your arms and legs at the same time. That's exactly what I need. Once I get one of those, it will help me a lot more.

When I first got injured, I was shipped to Spalding in Boston. They have everything you need. If I could get the money up, I would go right back there and continue working out.

I don't even know the price of the therapy, because it's handled privately through insurance payments. Insurance has to pay for it.

Hopefully everything will go right with this book, and I will be able to pay my way through it.

Currently, I exercise every day. I work out through range of motion. I have a couple people that come see me every day that help me out. I try to stay as fit as possible. I eat really good.

There was one girl that actually stuck with me through all of this. Nicole Maisonet. She helps me to this day. She helps me out a lot. She was my girlfriend, and she was there with me through thick and thin. She was the one that would get that title of being someone I would settle down for. When I got shot, she called me immediately and never left my side. I give her mad respect and props. She's still around. That's real love.

My current state of mind is this:

I don't count nothing out. Never counting nothing out.

There's so much more I could do on this earth that will serve a purpose.

Before You Go...

If you enjoyed reading my story, I would love to hear from you. Please take a brief moment to leave a review on Amazon so that this book will get into more hands. Every bit of exposure helps, and I am hoping that my story can be used to help bring about positive change for myself and my community. So please leave a brief review.

Thank you for your support.

Sincerely,
Mike Vaz

About the Author

Hailed as a local legend by his community, Mike Vaz is no stranger to success. He is a member of the Springfield Public High Schools Sports Hall of Fame for the incredible feats he accomplished during his football and basketball careers.

These achievements include being a three-time Super Bowl champ and earning the title of Western Mass MVP for football, and being a four-year starter and three-time All-Western Mass Lahovich Award winner for basketball.

Mike is known not just in Massachusetts, but throughout the northeast as a phenomenal athlete. He currently resides in his hometown of Springfield Massachusetts.

You can connect with Mike via email at Mikevaz29@yahoo.com.

Made in the USA
Middletown, DE
03 October 2020

20953010R00071